D0192883

FANTASY CROSS STITCH

JULIE HASLER'S

FANTASY CROSS STITCH

ZODIAC SIGNS, MYTHICAL BEASTS AND MYSTICAL CHARACTERS

David & Charles

A DAVID & CHARLES BOOK

First published in the UK in 1997
Reprinted in 1998
Text and designs © Copyright Julie Hasler 1997
Photography and layout Copyright © David & Charles 1997

Julie Hasler has asserted her right to be identified as author of this work
in accordance with the Copyright, Designs and Patents Act, 1988.

The designs in this book are copyright and must not be stitched for resale.

All rights reserved. No part of this publication may be reproduced, stored
in a retrieval system, or transmitted, in any form or by any means, electronic
or mechanical, by photocopying, recording or otherwise, without prior
permission in writing from the publisher.

A catalogue record for this book is available from the British Library.

ISBN 0 7153 0571 9

Photography by Jon and Barbara Stewart
Book design by Anita Ruddell
Printed in Italy by New Interlitho SpA
for David & Charles
Brunel House   Newton Abbot   Devon

*Previous page Aries the ram taken from the charted border
design on page 21 and embroidered on 18-count Aida fabric
using two strands of stranded cotton.*

Contents

Introduction

Fantasy – the very word conjures up mystery and excitement, dreams and desires. It tantalises and intrigues, inviting you to step out of the real world and experience the sensational realm of the Unknown.

It isn't a word you'd usually associate with cross stitch. Most designs reflect the reality we know – somewhat stylised at times, but mainly they deal with the everyday. But I wanted to do something different, something unexpected, to take cross stitch into new and unexplored dimensions. So, in *Fantasy Cross Stitch* you'll find a multitude of mythological deities, monsters and heroes, ancient legends and astrological symbols – fantastic images that have influenced mankind through the centuries.

These are not just enduring, powerful images; they are beautiful in their own right, and they are extremely versatile. As well as each main design, there are border and small scale designs which can be quickly worked into cards and small gifts. The Symbol Library on pages 112 to 121 is a collection of fascinating motifs and icons from different eras and beliefs all over the world. Either work the projects straight from the book or use your initiative to create your own by combining motifs from different charts and experimenting with colourways, to make designs that are uniquely yours.

This fantasy theme is a gold mine for unusual designs (particularly if you're looking for something to stitch for younger members of your family), and will appeal not only to younger stitchers, but also to anyone interested in the many ways our ancestors have tried to make sense of the world in which they lived.

The Pegasus and Unicorn cushions. Instructions for making these projects are given on pages 56–63.

Materials, Equipment and Techniques

This chapter gives you all the information you need to work the Fantasy Cross Stitch projects. It details the fabrics, threads and equipment you'll use, describes the stitches and techniques you'll need, and gives hints and tips for successfully creating these beautiful and mystical designs.

THE THINGS YOU NEED

NEEDLES
Use a small blunt tapestry needle: No 24 for fabrics up to 14-count, and No 26 for 16-count and finer work.

FABRIC
Evenweave fabrics such as Aida, Hardanger, Linda and linen, on which it is easy to count the threads, are used for cross stitch. The fabrics are woven so that there are the same number of threads per inch vertically and horizontally, letting you work cross stitches of equal height and width. Aida is woven as blocks: work one cross stitch over each block. Hardanger is woven as pairs of threads: work one cross stitch over two pairs of threads in each direction. Linda and linen are woven as single threads: work one cross stitch over two threads in each direction.

Evenweaves come in varying thread counts – that is, there is a choice in the number of threads, or blocks, per inch. For example, 14-count Aida has fourteen blocks to the inch, giving fourteen stitches to the inch. However, 12-count Aida has only twelve blocks per inch, giving twelve stitches to the inch. A design worked on 14-count Aida will be smaller than the same design worked on 12-count Aida. 28-count

Linda or linen both have twenty-eight threads to the inch, but as you usually work single cross stitches over pairs of threads, this gives fourteen stitches to the inch. So a design worked on 27-count Linda will be the same size as when worked on 14-count Aida.

These fabrics are all available in a wide choice of colours – white, ecru, black, red, blue, green and yellow to name but a few. The type of fabric to use is given with each project. Do not use a fabric which does not have an even weave, as this will distort the embroidery either horizontally or vertically.

If you want to stitch a design on a non-evenweave, disposable waste canvas has made stitching designs on to all kinds of materials so simple that it is tempting to use it on everything. Try adding designs to clothing, bed linen, curtains, tie-backs, bags - the list is endless. The only extra items you will need are a pair of fine tweezers, and a spray-bottle of water. See the Sagittarius project for detailed instructions.

THREADS
The designs in this book have been created using DMC six-stranded embroidery cottons (floss). The number of strands you use will depend upon the fabric you decide to work on. Details are given with each project, but generally, three strands are used for 11-count fabric, two

strands for 14, 16 and 18-count fabric, and one strand for 22-count and finer work.

When working with stranded cotton (floss), always separate the strands and place them together again before threading your needle and beginning to stitch. Never double the thread. For example, if you need to use two strands, use two separate strands, not one doubled-up. These simple steps will allow for much better coverage of the fabric, giving a neater finish.

DMC non-divisible gold and silver threads are to be used straight from the reel.

Kreinik blending filament has also been used for some of the designs. This can be used in conjunction with other threads to highlight areas, and add texture. The different fibres have different degrees of elasticity and control is essential, so follow the instructions below to knot the blending filament on the needle first, and then add the other thread.

1 Loop the filament and pass the loop through the eye of the needle, leaving a short tail.

2 Pass the loop of filament over the end of the needle.

3 Carefully tighten the filament loop at the end of the eye.

4 Gently stroke the knotted filament once to 'lock' it in place.

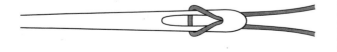

EMBROIDERY HOOPS

Embroidery hoops hold your fabric taut, and this tension makes stitching easier, enabling the needle to be pushed through the holes without piercing the fibres of the fabric. Wooden hoops with a screw-type tension adjuster, or round plastic hoops, in sizes 10cm (4in), 12.5cm (5in) or 15cm (6in) are ideal.

Large projects, such as the Wizard throw, can be worked by moving an embroidery hoop around the fabric as you progress. However, you might find it easier to use a larger, rectangular frame that takes most of the fabric.

SCISSORS

You'll need a pair of sharp embroidery scissors - these are essential, especially if a mistake has to be cut out - and a pair of dressmaking scissors to cut the fabric.

GOLD RELIEF OUTLINER

Gold relief outliner, available from art shops and good craft suppliers (see suppliers list on page 127), is usually used in glass painting. I've used it here in a number of projects to enhance various trimmings and craft jewels, and to decorate frames. It is very easy to use - just hold the tube at an angle like a pen with the nozzle resting lightly on the surface, and squeeze gently. When you have finished, place the work somewhere warm and dust-free to dry for a couple of hours; an airing cupboard is ideal.

PREPARING TO WORK

To prevent the fabric fraying, either hem, whip-stitch or machine stitch the edges, or cover them with a fold of masking tape. This helps keep the fabric neat and avoids loose fabric threads becoming tangled with your embroidery threads.

MAKING A START

It is preferable to begin cross stitch at the top of the design and work downwards. That way complex designs are easier to follow, and you can cross off completed rows on the chart as you finish them.

Where you make your first stitch is important as this will position the finished design on your fabric. First, find the exact centre point of the chart by following the arrows on the chart to their intersection. Next, locate the centre of your fabric by folding it in half vertically and then hor-izontally, pinching along the folds. Mark along these lines with tacking (basting) stitches if you prefer. The centre stitch of your design will be where the folds in the fabric meet.

To locate the starting point at the top, count the squares up from the centre of the chart, then count left or right to the first symbol. Next, count the corresponding number of holes up and across from the centre of the fabric and begin stitching at that point. Remember that each square on the chart represents a cross stitch on the fabric.

USING A HOOP

Place the area of fabric to be embroidered over the inner ring and carefully push the outer ring over it. Gently and evenly pull the fabric ensuring that it is drum taut in the hoop and the mesh is straight, tightening the screw adjuster as you go. When working, you will find it easier to have the screw in the 'ten-o-clock' position if you are right-handed, or in the 'one-o-clock' position if you are left-handed – this will prevent your thread from becoming tangled in the screw as you stitch.

While working you will find it necessary to retighten the hoop from time to time to keep the fabric taut.

THE STITCHES

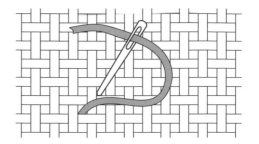

CROSS STITCH

To begin the stitch, bring the needle up from the wrong side, through a hole in the fabric at the left end of a row of stitches of the same colour (see diagram above).

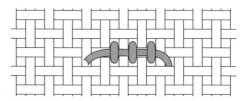

Fasten the thread by holding a short length of thread on the underside of the fabric, securing it with the first two or three stitches made (see diagram above). Never use knots as this will create a bumpy back surface and prevent your work from laying flat when completed.

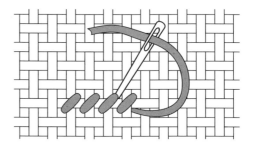

Next, bring the needle across one square (or block) to the right and one square (or block) above on a left-to-right diagonal and insert the needle (see diagram above). Half of the stitch is now completed. Continue in this way until the end of the row is reached. Your stitches should be diagonal on the right side of the fabric and vertical on the wrong side.

Complete the upper half of the stitch by crossing back from right to left to form an 'X'. Work all the stitches in the row by completing all

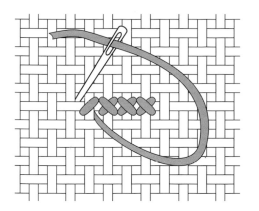

the X's (see diagram above). The diagram below shows how to work vertical rows.

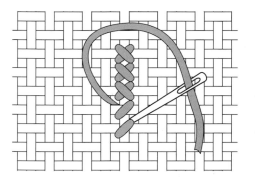

Cross stitch can also be worked by crossing each stitch as you come to it, as you would do for isolated stitches. This method works just as well as the previous one; which method you use is really a personal preference.

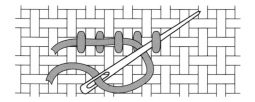

Finish all threads by running your needle under four or more stitches on the wrong side of the work (see diagram above) and cut close.

BASIC BACKSTITCH

Basic backstitch is used in some of the designs, mainly for outlines and finer details. Always work any backstitch when your cross stitch embroidery has been completed, using one strand fewer than that used in the embroidery. For example, if three strands of stranded cotton (floss) have been used to work the cross stitch embroidery, use two strands for the backstitching. If only one strand of stranded cotton is used to work the

cross stitch embroidery, one strand is also used for the backstitching.

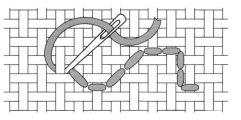

Backstitch is worked from hole to hole and can be stitched in diagonal, vertical or horizontal lines (see diagram above). Always take care not to pull the stitches too tight, otherwise the contrast of colour will be lost against the cross stitches. Finish off the threads as for cross stitch.

Useful Tips

1 When you are stitching, it is important not to pull the fabric out of shape. Work the stitches in two motions, straight up through a hole in the fabric and then straight down ensuring the fabric remains taut. Make sure that you don't pull the thread tight – snug, but not tight. If you use this method, you will find that the thread will lie just where you want it to and not pull your fabric out of shape.

2 If your thread becomes twisted while working, drop your needle and let it hang down freely. It will then untwist itself. Do not continue working with twisted thread as it will appear thinner and not cover your fabric as well.

3 Never leave your needle in the design area of your work when not in use. No matter how good the needle might be, it could rust in time, and may mark your work permanently.

4 Do not carry thread across an open expanse of fabric. If you are working separate areas of the same colour, finish off and begin again. Loose threads, especially dark colours, will be visible from the right side of your work when the project is completed.

Celestial Heavens

*T*he world has ever been an uncertain place, and people have constantly striven to make sense of it. For thousands of years they looked to Astrology for help and guidance, interpreting the movements of the planets and the stars to discover their destinies.

The projects in this section are all inspired by the power and vitality of Astrology. The twelve signs of the zodiac are represented by extremely visual and colourful designs, each accompanied by a simple border featuring small motifs. Within each individual sign, they offer endless scope. The projects explore different settings for the zodiac designs – some are worked as window-hangings, some as cards or framed pictures; but don't stick with the combinations you see – all the designs work beautifully in all settings.

For the final two projects, exquisite designs feature the sun and moon, and the ruling planets. Popular belief decrees that these planets affect our temperament and our character, depending on our date and time of birth. You will also find special astrological symbols representing each planet, and stylised images characterising individual signs, such as a goat-fish for Capricorn, a centaur-bowman for Sagittarius and the crab for Cancer.

Whether you take these ancient beliefs seriously or not, all these images are fascinating and make beautiful designs in their own right.

Aquarius the Water-bearer

21 January – 19 February

The ancient Egyptians linked Aquarius with Hapi the Nile God who, when the river overflowed each year, brought life to their kingdom. To the Greeks, Aquarius was Ganymede, the most beautiful youth in creation, carried off by an eagle to become Zeus' cup-bearer. In ancient art, Aquarius is often depicted as an angel, freely pouring out living water for all mankind.

✱ Aquarius' ruling planets are Uranus and Saturn. The Aquarian personality is unconventional, humanitarian, constructive, artistic, tenacious and intuitive, with a drive towards a detached, if original, pursuit of truth. Gregarious and clear-sighted, under pressure Aquarians tend to be unpredictable, self-centred and perverse. They can become fanatical, tactless and rebellious.

Zodiac Window Hanging

The flexibility and strength of perforated paper make it the perfect medium for working your zodiac sign as a window hanging. Add decorative craft accessories such as bells, chimes and jewels using, perhaps, the colours and gemstones traditionally associated with the sign (see page 34). For a list of the materials required, refer to page 16.

1 Find the starting point on the perforated paper (see page 10) and, following the Aquarius chart opposite, work the design downwards. Use two strands of stranded cotton (floss) and the fil or clair gold thread straight from the reel. Remember to handle the perforated paper with care, and try not to bend it while stitching.

2 When you have completed the embroidery, place it face down on a soft cloth or towel and iron the interfacing on to the wrong side of the work to give it added strength.

3 Place the work face up on a firm, flat surface, and position the jewellery stones on the perforated paper, as close to the edge of the embroidery as possible. Glue them in place with craft adhesive. Put aside and leave to dry.

4 Decide on the position, length and number of each collection of hanging bells, beads or chimes. For each selection, cut approximately 50.5cm (20in) of the fil or mi-fin gold thread, and thread your chosen items on to it before doubling it up in the needle. Push the needle firmly through the work from the back, and pull the gold thread through until it reaches the desired length. Remove the needle, and temporarily fix the loose ends of thread to the interfacing with a piece of masking tape.

5 When you have done this for each length and for the central hanging loop at the top, turn the work over so that the wrong side is facing you and brush craft adhesive over the gold thread ends, removing the masking tape when thoroughly dry.

6 Outline the design with the gold relief outliner, as detailed on page 9. Leave to dry.

7 Cut out the design with the scalpel or craft knife, cutting as close as possible to the gold outline. Be careful not to cut through the gold thread. Squeeze a little of the gold relief outliner into a small container, and brush around the edges of the design to cover up the raw edges.

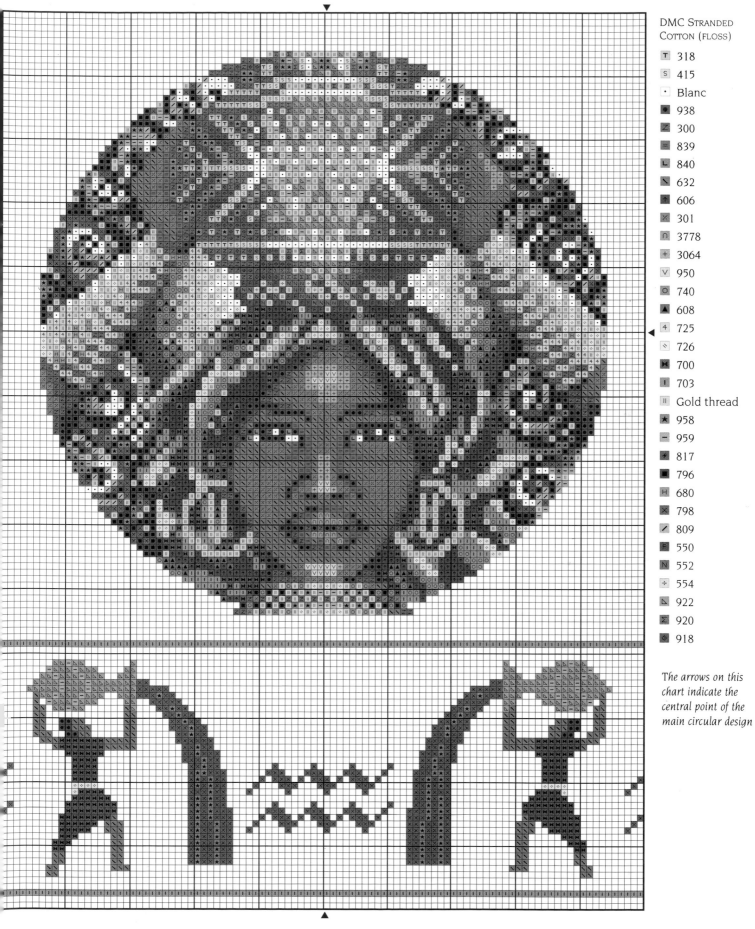

DMC STRANDED
COTTON (FLOSS)

T	318
S	415
·	Blanc
⊛	938
Z	300
=	839
L	840
◰	632
⬆	606
⊠	301
∩	3778
+	3064
V	950
O	740
▲	608
＋	725
⬙	726
⋈	700
I	703
‖	Gold thread
★	958
−	959
⚡	817
■	796
H	680
⊠	798
⁄	809
⊞	550
N	552
÷	554
◺	922
Σ	920
⊛	918

*The arrows on this
chart indicate the
central point of the
main circular design*

15

Pisces the Fish

20 FEBRUARY – 20 MARCH

According to the ancient Greeks, the stars of the constellation Pisces are the fish that saved Aphrodite and Eros from the turbulent Euphrates, placed in the heavens by the grateful goddess. The Fish has long been an emotive sign, and was taken up by the early Christians as a secret symbol of Christ. The symbolism is particularly appropriate for the ritual of baptism by water.

✱ Pisces' ruling planets are Neptune and Jupiter. Mystical, talented and peace-loving, Pisceans have vivid imaginations and a strong spiritual sensitivity. Deeply intuitive, their conviviality makes them charming companions. Pisceans often find it difficult to make decisions or solve practical problems, and can retreat from reality into their own dream world. Unable to commit themselves, they may drift from one interest to another.

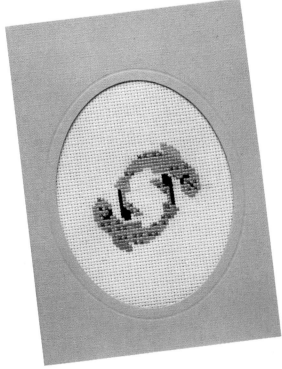

Take any star sign from its zodiac border, embroider it on 18-count Aida fabric using two strands of stranded cotton (floss); set in a DMC greetings card blank. To assemble the card, see 'Displaying Your Work', page 123.

ZODIAC WINDOW HANGING

Although Pisces makes a particularly perfect window hanging, with the twin fish swimming lazily through the light, all the zodiac designs translate into stunning hangings. Simply follow your chosen zodiac chart, using the stitching and making up instructions for Aquarius on page 14 with the materials listed below.

✱ Mill Hill gold 14-count perforated needlework paper, one 23 x 30.5cm (9 x 12in) sheet
✱ Heavy-weight iron-on interfacing, slightly smaller than the perforated paper
✱ DMC stranded cotton (floss) in the colours listed on the chart
✱ DMC fil or clair light gold thread
✱ DMC fil or mi-fin gold thread
✱ Tapestry needle, No 24
✱ Craft adhesive
✱ Masking tape
✱ Scalpel or craft knife
✱ Small watercolour paintbrush
✱ Tube of gold relief outliner
✱ Jewellery stones of your choice
✱ Various items to hang from the design, such as bells, chimes and beads

Photographed on pages 18–19, the Cancer, Aquarius and Pisces window hangings. Each displays the range of decorative possibilities open to you.

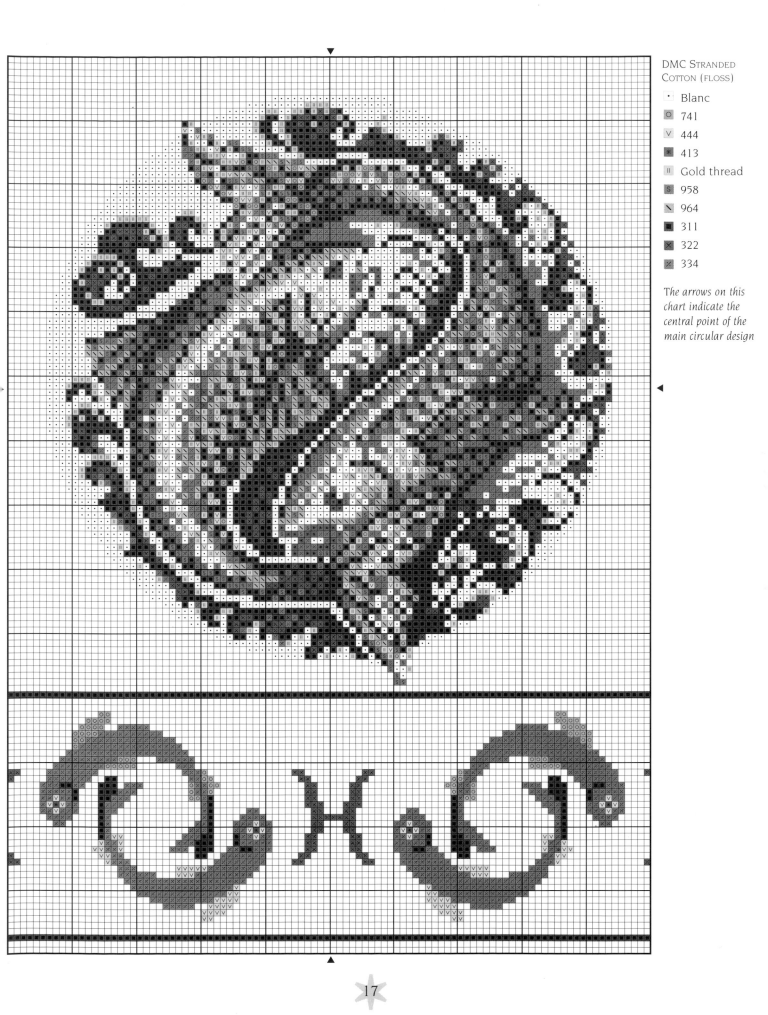

DMC STRANDED
COTTON (FLOSS)

- Blanc
- 741
- 444
- 413
- Gold thread
- 958
- 964
- 311
- 322
- 334

The arrows on this chart indicate the central point of the main circular design

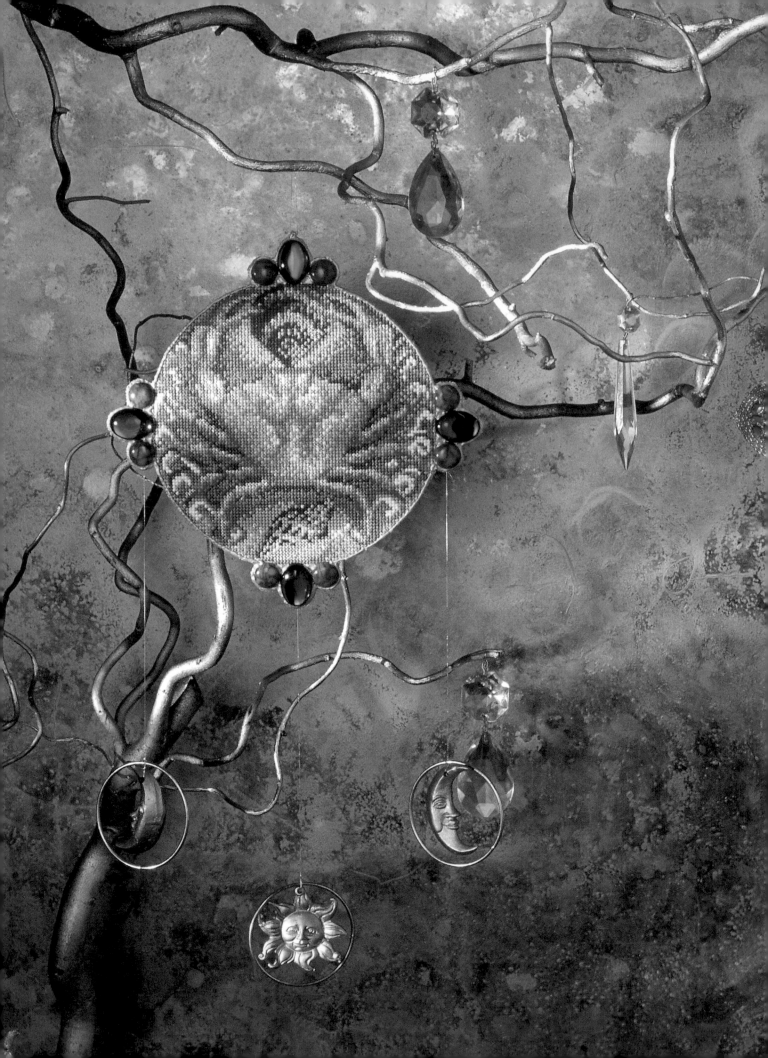

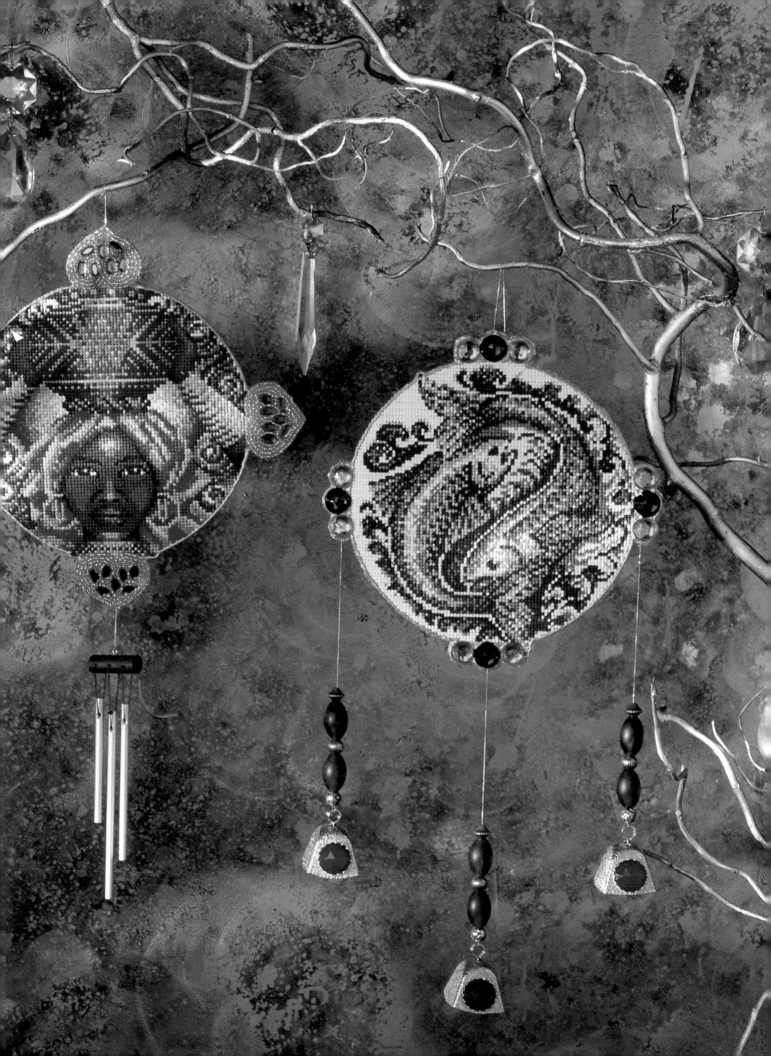

Aries the Ram

21 March – 20 April

Greek myth tells how Phrixus, son of king Athamas, was spirited away from Thessaly on the back of a ram with a golden fleece. When he arrived safely in Colchis, he sacrificed the ram to Zeus, who placed it in the heavens as the constellation Aries. Its golden fleece was famously recovered by Jason, leader of the Argonauts.

✱ Aries' ruling planet is Mars. True to the Fire element, Arieans are assertive and outgoing, courageous and fierce-tempered. They like excitement and variety, and often seem to be in a hurry. They enjoy competition, but often lose interest in lengthy, time-consuming tasks. Under pressure, they tend to be selfish, egotistical, impatient, overbearing and argumentative.

Zodiac Decorated Card

What could be more appropriate for zodiac designs than to make them into birthday cards? There are many commercially made cards available (see page 123 for instructions on mounting embroidery into cards), but with just a little ingenuity you can create your own exceptional versions. Stencils and gold spray paint have transformed the simple black card surround for Aries; see Libra and Scorpio, pictured on pages 36 and 37, for more ideas.

1 For the materials you will need for this card, see page 38. Substitute gold spray paint (car paint is ideal) for the gold pen. Prepare your fabric, find the starting point (see page 10) then, following the Aries chart opposite, work the design downwards. Use one strand of stranded cotton (floss).

2 When you have completed the embroidery, place it face down on a soft cloth or towel and press it (see page 122). Then, iron the interfacing on to the wrong side to add strength.

3 Make a fold-line dividing the thick black card into two equal sections by measuring 28cm (11in) along the width and lightly marking a line on the wrong side. Using the scalpel or craft knife, cut an aperture 15cm (6in) square from the left-hand section. With the back of the blade, gently score the fold-line previously marked.

4 Make a stencil out of the sheet of thin card. Sketch a series of abstract patterns on to the card, and cut them out.

5 Next, cover a firm, flat surface in newspaper, and place the thick black card face up on to it. Cover any area you don't want to decorate with a piece of scrap paper. Move your stencil around until you see a shape that suits the area to be painted and, holding your stencil in one hand, spray lightly with the paint following the manufacturer's directions. Keep moving the stencil around until you have painted the entire area. Remove the scrap paper, and set the card aside to dry.

6 Turn your card over to the wrong side, and stick the double-sided adhesive tape all round the aperture. Place the embroidery face up on a clean, flat surface then take your card and position the aperture centrally over the embroidery. Press down firmly all round the window.

7 Turn your card over to the wrong side, and glue the piece of contrasting thin card over the back of the embroidery, using the adhesive. Fold the card in half along the scored line.

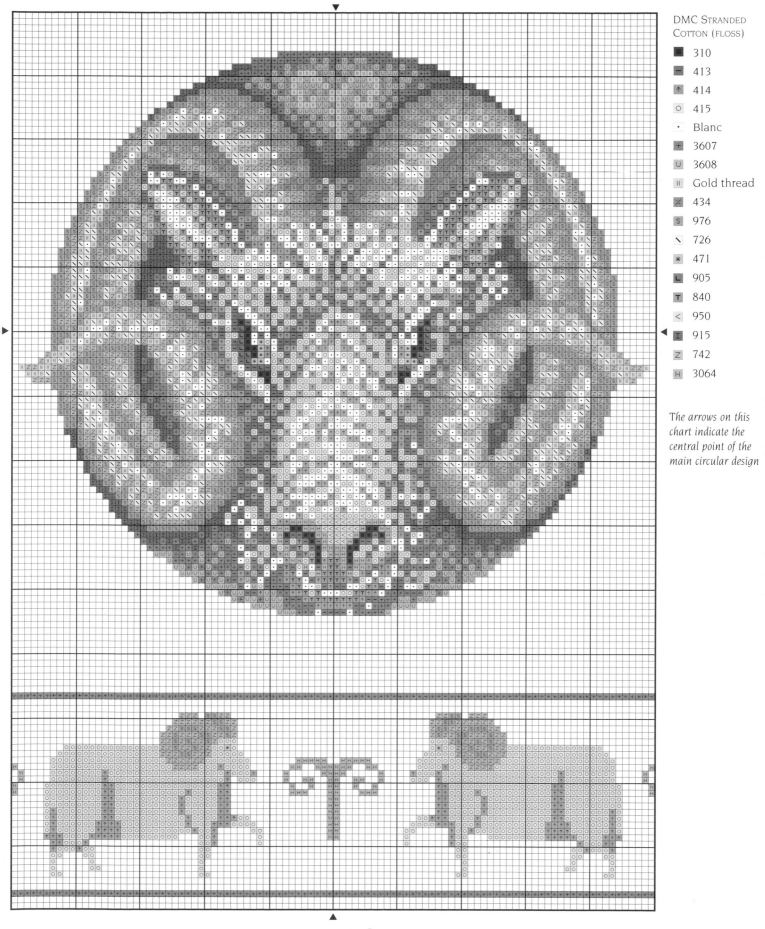

DMC Stranded
Cotton (floss)

■	310
−	413
↑	414
○	415
·	Blanc
+	3607
U	3608
‖	Gold thread
╱	434
S	976
╲	726
*	471
L	905
T	840
<	950
I	915
Z	742
H	3064

The arrows on this chart indicate the central point of the main circular design

Taurus the Bull

21 APRIL – 21 MAY

From earliest days, the bull has been a potent symbol of strength, fertility and growth. In Memphis, the Egyptians worshipped the Nile god, the supreme fertility deity, in the form of Apis the bull. Greek Zeus transformed himself into a white bull to abduct the beautiful Europa. In Persian astrology the name of the Heavenly Bull meant 'Bull of Light'.

✳ Taurus' ruling planet is Venus. The Taurean personality is grounded and down-to-earth – strong-willed, conservative, practical, reliable, businesslike and patient. Taureans appreciate beauty and comfort, and can show creativity in music, words and painting. Although they are friendly and warm-hearted, they can be stubborn and tend to bear grudges.

DECORATED BOX LID

Whilst browsing through a gift shop, I was lucky enough to find a pretty hand-painted box (shown on page 12), which happened to be just the right size to mount a zodiac embroidery on to! With time and effort, any box can be decorated in this way, making an unusual birthday gift.

✳ Gold fleck Bellana fabric, 20-count, 16.5cm (6½in) square
✳ DMC stranded cotton (floss) in the colours listed on the chart
✳ DMC fil or clair light gold thread
✳ Tapestry needle, No 26
✳ Plain or decorated wooden box with a 14cm (5½in) square lid
✳ Forty-four brass upholstery tacks
✳ Small hammer
✳ Small amount of kapok

1 Prepare your fabric, find the starting point (see page 10) then, following the Taurus chart opposite, work the design downwards. Use one strand of stranded cotton (floss), and the fil or clair gold thread, which is not stranded, straight from the reel.

2 When you have completed the embroidery, place it face down on a soft cloth or towel and press it carefully (see page 122) turning over a 1.5cm (⅝in) seam allowance to the wrong side on all four raw edges.

3 To mount the embroidery on to the box lid, place the box on a firm, flat surface and position the embroidery face up on the lid. Gently tap in the upholstery tacks with the hammer, making sure they are evenly spaced and just slightly overlapping the edges of the fabric. Leave a 5cm (2in) gap on one side.

4 To pad the lid slightly, gently push the kapok under the fabric, using the end of a pen or pencil. Use a small piece at a time to get an even finish. Tap in the remaining upholstery tacks.

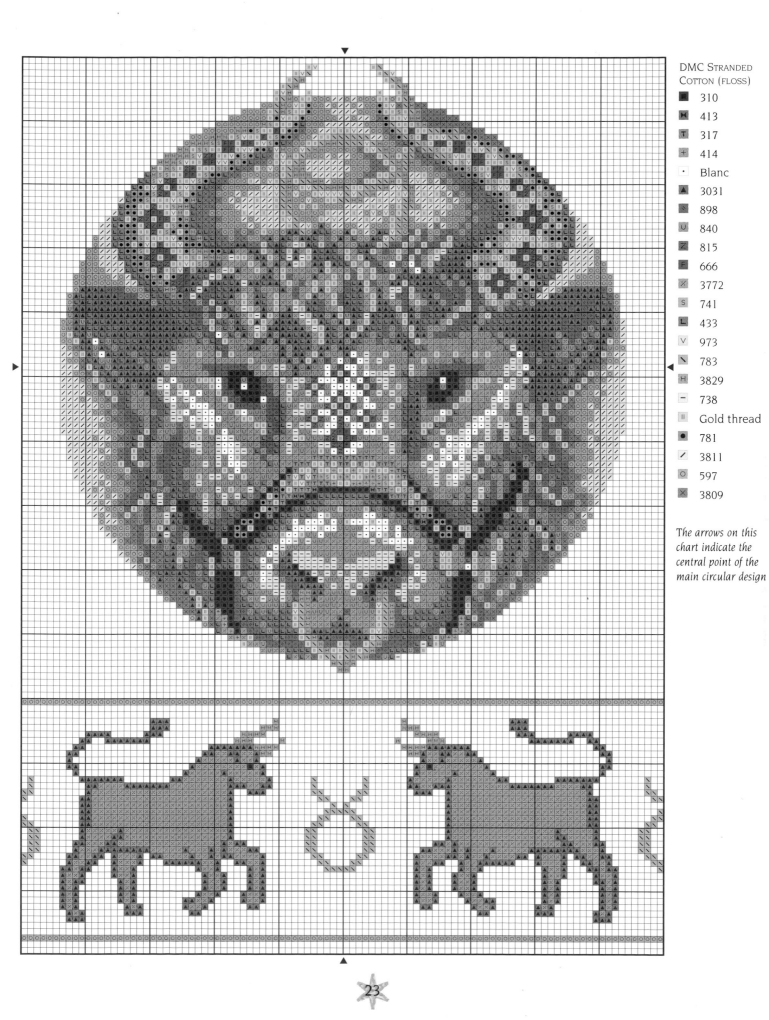

DMC STRANDED
COTTON (FLOSS)

■	310
⋈	413
T	317
+	414
·	Blanc
▲	3031
⊠	898
U	840
Z	815
F	666
⊠	3772
S	741
L	433
V	973
◺	783
H	3829
−	738
‖	Gold thread
●	781
╱	3811
O	597
⊠	3809

The arrows on this chart indicate the central point of the main circular design

Gemini the Twins

22 May – 21 June

The twin Greek heroes Kastor and Polydeukes (Castor and Pollux to the Romans) were the sons of Leda and Zeus. When Kastor was slain by his cousin, Polydeukes begged Zeus to let him die too. But Zeus decreed that they should spend their days alternatively in the Underworld and on Mount Olympus with the gods. He then set their image amongst the stars as Gemini.

✱ Gemini's ruling planet is Mercury. Idealistic, expressive and inquisitive, versatile Geminis have a two-sided personality. Because they can change moods quickly and see both sides of an argument they make excellent communicators. But the negative expression of the same traits can make them moody, changeable, superficial, restless, impatient and lacking in concentration.

ZODIAC JEWELLERY HANGER

The jewel-like zodiac designs look excellent framed as pictures – but why stop there? Add hooks to the frame and you have a very unusual – and practical – jewellery hanger to hang above your dressing table. This frame has six hooks attached to it – but you could add more or less, depending on the size of your frame. Use the hooks to display your necklaces and pendants, bracelets and brooches, or even your dangly earrings. You will never mislay your jewellery again!

- ✱ Navy 14-count Aida fabric, 35.5cm (14in) square
- ✱ DMC stranded cotton (floss) in the colours listed on the chart
- ✱ DMC fil or clair light gold thread
- ✱ Tapestry needle, No 24
- ✱ Firm mounting board, 25.5cm (10in) square
- ✱ Masking tape
- ✱ A picture frame of your choice
- ✱ Six 2.5cm (1in) round brass cup hooks
- ✱ Bradawl

1 Prepare your fabric, find the starting point (see page 10) then, following the Gemini chart on page 25, work the design downwards. Use two strands of stranded cotton (floss), and the fil or clair, which is not stranded, straight from the reel.

2 When you have completed the embroidery, place it face down on a soft cloth or towel and press it carefully (see page 122).

3 See 'Mounting embroideries for framing' on page 122 to mount and frame the finished embroidery, then simply attach the cup hooks to the frame in the desired positions. Make a small hole for each one with the bradawl, and screw them in gently by hand. Remember to space them evenly.

Photographed on page 26 *Gemini zodiac jewellery hanger and selection of zodiac jewellery. Framecraft silver plated and golden jewellery frames make excellent settings for the astrological symbols from the zodiac borders. Stitch your chosen symbol in DMC gold and silver thread on fine 22-count Hardanger fabric. To assemble the jewellery frames, see page 125. Hang them on leather thongs decorated with antique gold and silver-finish beads.*

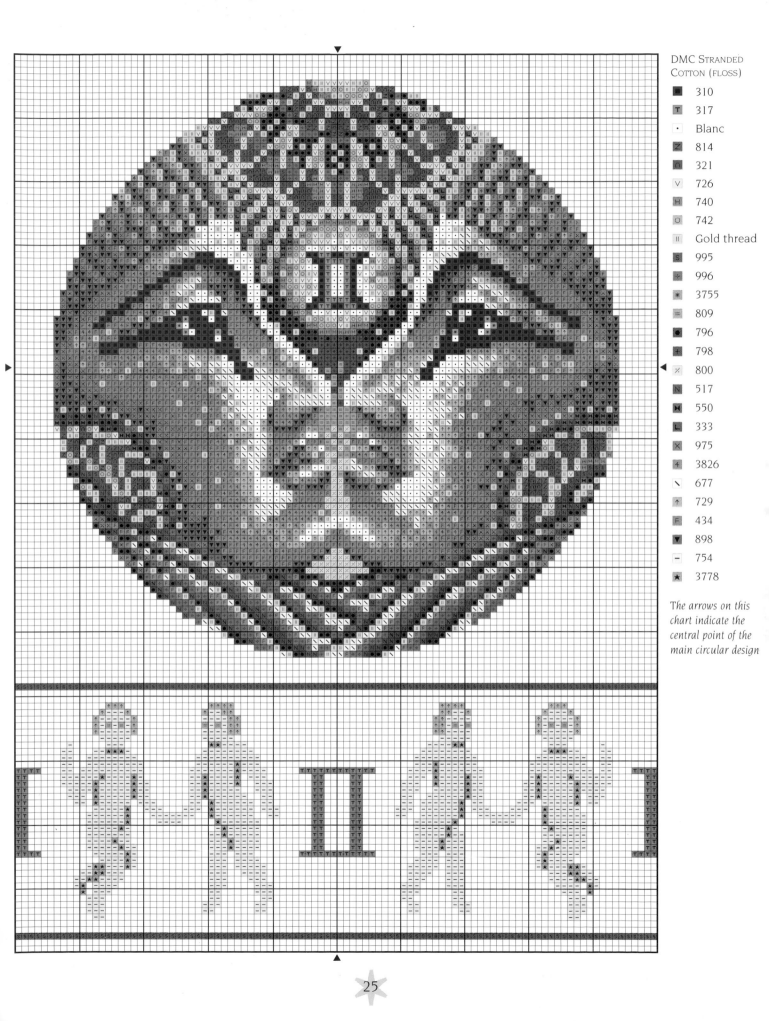

DMC Stranded
Cotton (floss)

■	310
T	317
·	Blanc
Z	814
⋒	321
V	726
H	740
O	742
‖	Gold thread
S	995
✦	996
✳	3755
=	809
●	796
✛	798
⁒	800
N	517
M	550
L	333
X	975
4	3826
＼	677
↑	729
F	434
▼	898
−	754
★	3778

The arrows on this chart indicate the central point of the main circular design

Cancer The Crab

22 June – 23 July

When Herakles fought the monstrous Hydra of Lerna, the goddess Hera sent Cancer to intervene. The giant crab bit the hero's foot, but was immediately crushed to death. Hera placed the image of her fallen champion amongst the stars of the zodiac.

✱ Cancer is connected with conception and birth, often referred to as 'The Gate of Birth'. Cancer's ruling planet is the Moon. The Cancerian personality is retiring, emotional and vulnerable, with a love of home and family life. Intuitive and artistic, Cancerians rely more on feelings than reason. Under pressure, they tend to become very timid, self-absorbed and intensely moody. They can be selfish and difficult to get on with.

The image of Cancer the Crab from the zodiac border on page 28, embroidered on 18-count sky blue Aida fabric using two strands of stranded cotton (floss), and set in the lid of a 7.5cm (3in) gilt metal miniature box. To assemble the box lid, see 'Displaying Your Work' on page 124.

Zodiac Window Hanging

The Cancer design has been made up into the third mystical window hanging.

Using the materials listed for the Pisces on page 16, simply stitch from the Cancer chart shown overleaf, following the stitching and making up instructions as given for Aquarius on page 14.

The Elements

Each zodiac sign falls under one of the four elements, taking its characteristics. According to Aristotle, these four elements are the general and essential elements of life. Plato stated that God used the four elements in the creation of the world.

Fire: Ardent and keen
Fire signs – Aries, Leo, Sagittarius

Earth: Practical and cautious
Earth signs – Taurus, Virgo, Capricorn

Air: Intellectual and communicative
Air signs – Aquarius, Gemini, Libra

Water: Emotional and sensitive
Water signs – Pisces, Cancer, Scorpio

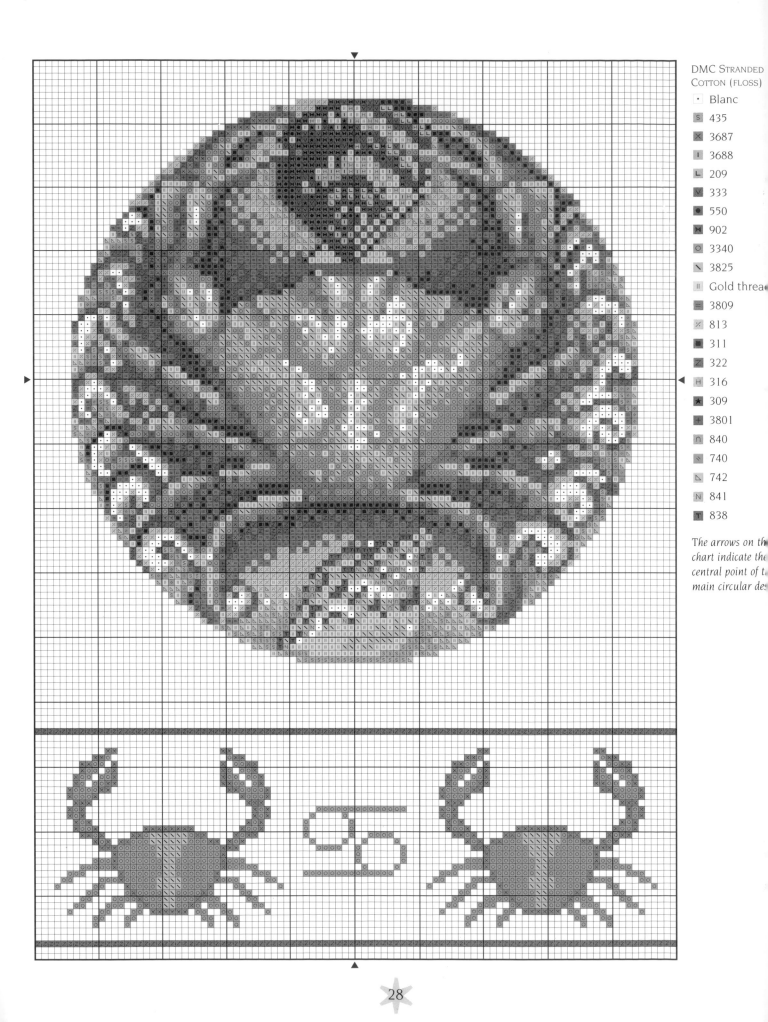

DMC STRANDED
COTTON (FLOSS)

·	Blanc
S	435
✕	3687
I	3688
L	209
V	333
●	550
⋈	902
○	3340
╲	3825
‖	Gold thread
≡	3809
⁄	813
■	311
Z	322
H	316
★	309
+	3801
⊓	840
⊠	740
⊿	742
N	841
T	838

The arrows on th
chart indicate the
central point of t
main circular des

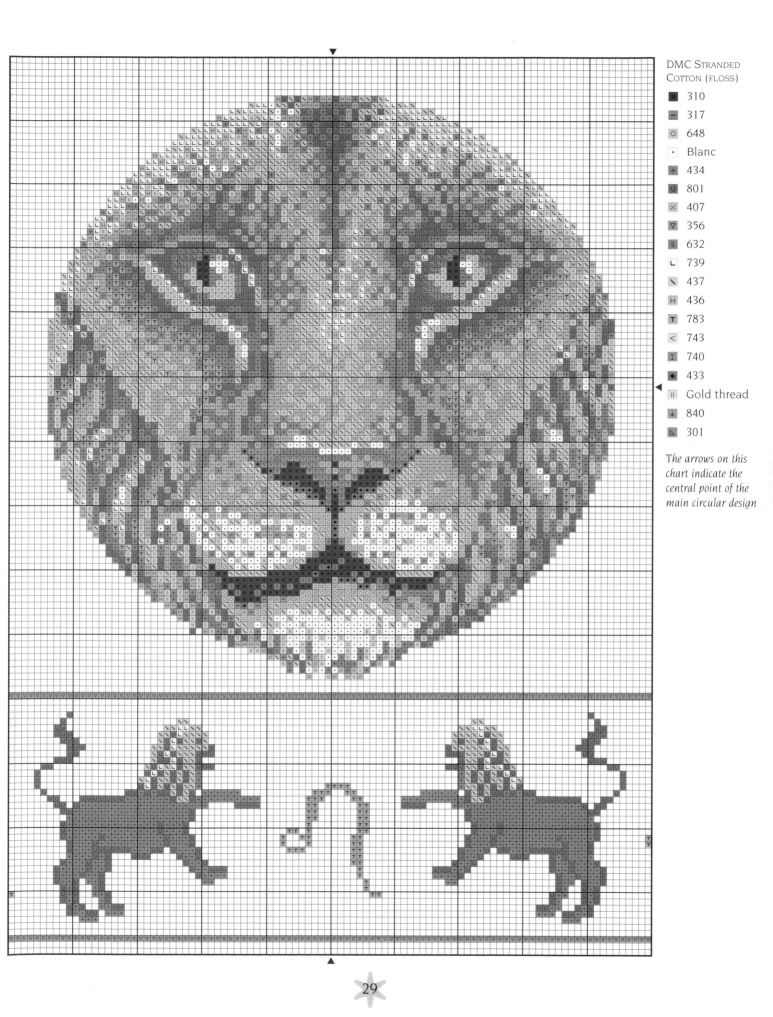

DMC Stranded
Cotton (floss)

- ■ 310
- − 317
- ○ 648
- · Blanc
- + 434
- U 801
- ⁄ 407
- ▽ 356
- S 632
- L 739
- \ 437
- H 436
- T 783
- < 743
- I 740
- ◆ 433
- ‖ Gold thread
- ↓ 840
- ◰ 301

The arrows on this chart indicate the central point of the main circular design

Leo the Lion

24 July – 23 August

The lion symbol for Leo goes back to the Babylonian zodiac when it was called 'the Great Light'. It is also associated with the Lion of Nemea, a ferocious beast which Herakles strangled with his bare hands. During the medieval period, Leo was often depicted with a sceptre and a sword, representing the capacity for good and evil.

✷ Leo's ruling planet is the Sun. Traditionally linked with kings, Leo's regal nature is exuberant, proud, and strong willed. Self-expressive, authoritative and flamboyant (in fact, often quite theatrical), Leos enjoy being the centre of attention. However, they can be too proud, and under pressure may become domineering, pompous and predatory.

Zodiac Hand Painted Frame

Ordinary ready-made frames can often be dramatically improved with just a touch of paint and a little creativity. For my Leo picture I used black paint on a gold frame, matching the Aida fabric and reinforcing Leo's affinity with sun colours. If you stitch a different zodiac sign, decorate the frame with its traditional colours – see page 34.

✷ Black Aida fabric, 14-count, 35.5cm (14in) square
✷ DMC stranded cotton (floss) in the colours listed on the chart
✷ DMC fil or clair light gold thread
✷ Tapestry needle, No 24
✷ Firm mounting board, 25.5 cm (10in) square
✷ Masking tape
✷ A picture frame of your choice
✷ Scrap paper, 25.5cm (10in) square
✷ A sheet of thin card (card of various sorts is available from art shops or good stationers)
✷ Scalpel or craft knife
✷ A can of spray paint in a colour of your choice (car paint is ideal)

1 Prepare your fabric, find the starting point (see page 10) then, following the Leo chart on page 29, work the design downwards. Use two strands of stranded cotton (floss), and the fil or clair gold thread, which is not stranded, straight from the reel.

2 When you have completed the embroidery, place it face down on a soft cloth or towel and press it carefully (see page 122).

3 See 'Mounting embroideries for framing' on page 122 to mount and frame the finished embroidery.

4 Make a stencil out of the sheet of thin card. Sketch a series of abstract patterns on to the card with a soft pencil, and cut them out with the scalpel or craft knife.

5 Next, cover a firm, flat surface in newspaper, and place the framed picture on to it. Cover the glazed area of the frame with the 25.5cm (10in) square of scrap paper to mask it from the paint. Move your stencil around until you see a shape that suits the area of frame to be painted, and holding your stencil in one hand, spray lightly with the paint following the manufacturer's directions. Move the stencil round the frame until you have painted the entire frame. Remove the scrap paper and set aside to dry.

Photographed opposite, the Leo and Virgo designs have been worked as framed pictures. With a little creativity, a simple ready-made frame can be transformed into the perfect setting for your embroidery.

Virgo the Virgin

24 AUGUST – 23 SEPTEMBER

With Virgo covering the time of the harvest, it is no surprise that the sign has often been associated with harvest maidens and fertility goddesses. Demeter, goddess of the fruits and riches of the soil, and her daughter Persephone were often linked with Virgo, as was Ishtar, the great earth-mother, fertility goddess. In Christianity, Virgo is associated with the Virgin Mary.

✱ Virgo's ruling planet is Mercury. Typical Virgoans are intelligent and practical, liking order and tidiness in all things. Good at concentrating on detail, they rely on reason rather than emotion. They are not natural leaders, so they tend to work in the background where they often become very powerful. Their character runs the risk of appearing unsympathetic and too proud, and under pressure, they tend to be hypocritical, fastidious and finicky.

ZODIAC PICTURE WITH HAND-DECORATED FRAME

The gold relief effect I've used is really easy to achieve, and turns an ordinary gold frame into something special. You don't need to add a lot of decoration – just as much or as little as you want. And it doesn't have to be complicated either, as just a few well placed lines can create a stunning effect. All you need is a bit of imagination and you will have a picture to be really proud of!

✱ Black Aida fabric, 14-count, 35.5cm (14in) square
✱ DMC stranded cotton (floss) in the colours listed on the chart
✱ DMC fil or clair light gold thread
✱ Tapestry needle, No 24
✱ Firm mounting board, 25.5cm (10in) square
✱ Masking tape
✱ A picture frame of your choice
✱ Tube of gold relief outliner

1 Prepare your fabric, find the starting point (see page 10) then, following the Virgo chart opposite, work the design downwards. Use two strands of stranded cotton (floss), and the fil or clair gold thread, which is not stranded, straight from the reel.

2 When you have completed the embroidery, place it face down on a soft cloth or towel and press it carefully (see page 122).

3 See 'Mounting embroideries for framing' on page 122 to mount and frame the finished embroidery.

4 Place the framed picture on a firm, flat surface, and carefully decorate it using the gold relief outliner following instructions on page 9. Abstract shapes and patterns are easier to work, as you don't have to work out measurements! Leave to dry.

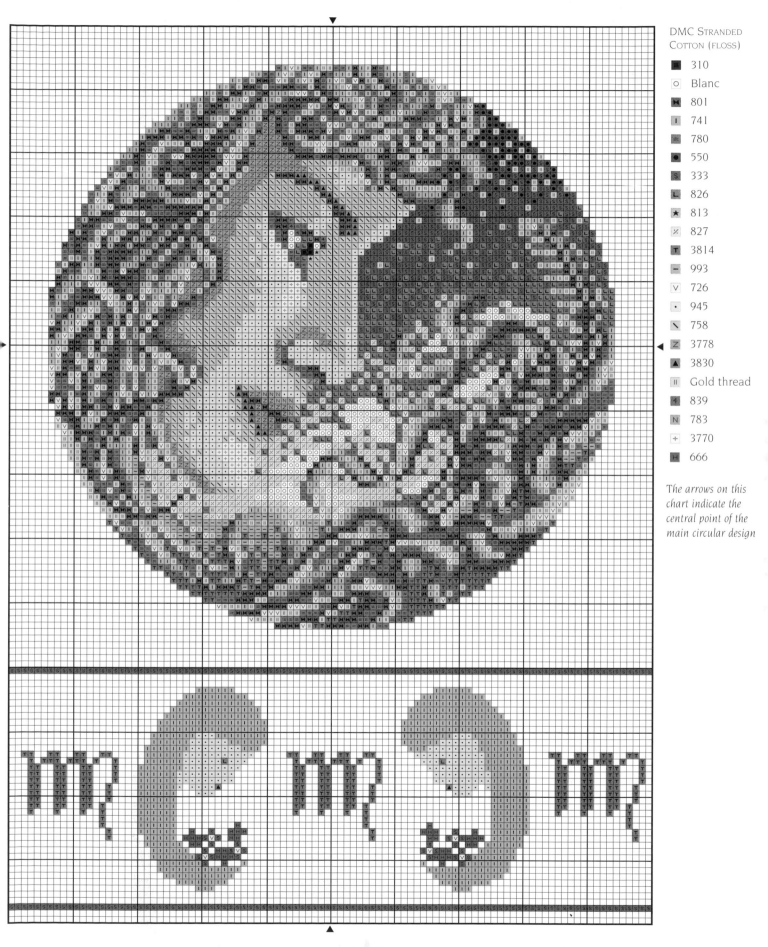

DMC STRANDED
COTTON (FLOSS)

- 310
○ Blanc
- 801
I 741
= 780
● 550
S 333
L 826
★ 813
✕ 827
T 3814
- 993
V 726
· 945
\ 758
Z 3778
▲ 3830
‖ Gold thread
839
N 783
÷ 3770
H 666

*The arrows on this
chart indicate the
central point of the
main circular design*

33

Libra the Balance

24 September – 23 October

A sign of justice, diplomacy and the arts, Libra has long been associated with the concept of balance and equilibrium. The ancient Greeks associated Libra with Mochis, the legendary inventor of weights and measures – particularly fitting as Libra's span covers the time of weighing the harvest. Libra was also connected with the Roman goddess of justice, Astraea, balancing the Scales of Justice.

✱ Libra's ruling planet is Venus. The Libran nature is gentle, discriminative, sensitive, liking balance and harmony, disliking conflict and sudden change. Warm, friendly and sociable, Librans are usually good at patching up quarrels for others. Under pressure, however, the sense of balance tends to be lost, and the impractical side becomes emphasised. There may be a tendency for the Libran to become passive, lazy, indecisive, resentful, frivolous and gullible.

Zodiac Decorated Card

To make this card, follow the Libra chart opposite and refer to page 38 for a list of materials and general instructions on how to make the card. Cut an aperture that is at least 20.5cm (8in) wide in the mount, making it as ornate or plain as you wish. Finally, decorate it with jewellery stones in colours that compliment your embroidery.

Colours and Gemstones of the Zodiac

Traditionally, each zodiac sign has been associated with specific gemstones, metals and colours. Use this list to choose appropriate colours and metals to decorate your work.

AQUARIUS
Gemstone: Aquamarine
Metals: Uranium and aluminium
Colours: Aquamarine, turquoise and electric blue

PISCES
Gemstone: Amethyst
Metals: Germanium and strontium
Colours: Mauve, purple and violet, sea-green and silver

ARIES
Gemstone: Diamond
Metal: Iron
Colours: Red, scarlet and carmine

TAURUS
Gemstone: Emerald
Metal: Copper
Colours: Pale blue, yellow, pink and pale green

GEMINI
Gemstone: Agate
Metal: Quicksilver
Colours: Yellow, slate-grey and spotted mixtures

CANCER
Gemstones: Moonstone and pearl
Metal: Silver
Colours: White, opal, iridescent silvery hues, smoky grey, sea green and blue

LEO
Gemstone: Ruby
Metal: Gold
Colours: Orange, gold, rich shades of yellow, brown

VIRGO
Gemstone: Peridot
Metal: Quicksilver
Colours: Shades of green, dark brown, slate and spotted patterns

LIBRA
Gemstone: Opal
Metal: Copper
Colours: Lemon yellow, pale blue, pale green and pink

SCORPIO
Gemstones: Topaz and malachite
Metal: Plutonium
Colours: Dark red, maroon and smoky cloud formations

SAGITTARIUS
Gemstone: Turquoise
Metal: Tin
Colours: Rich purple, violet, red and indigo

CAPRICORN
Gemstone: Garnet
Metal: Lead
Colours: Dark grey, black, dark brown and indigo

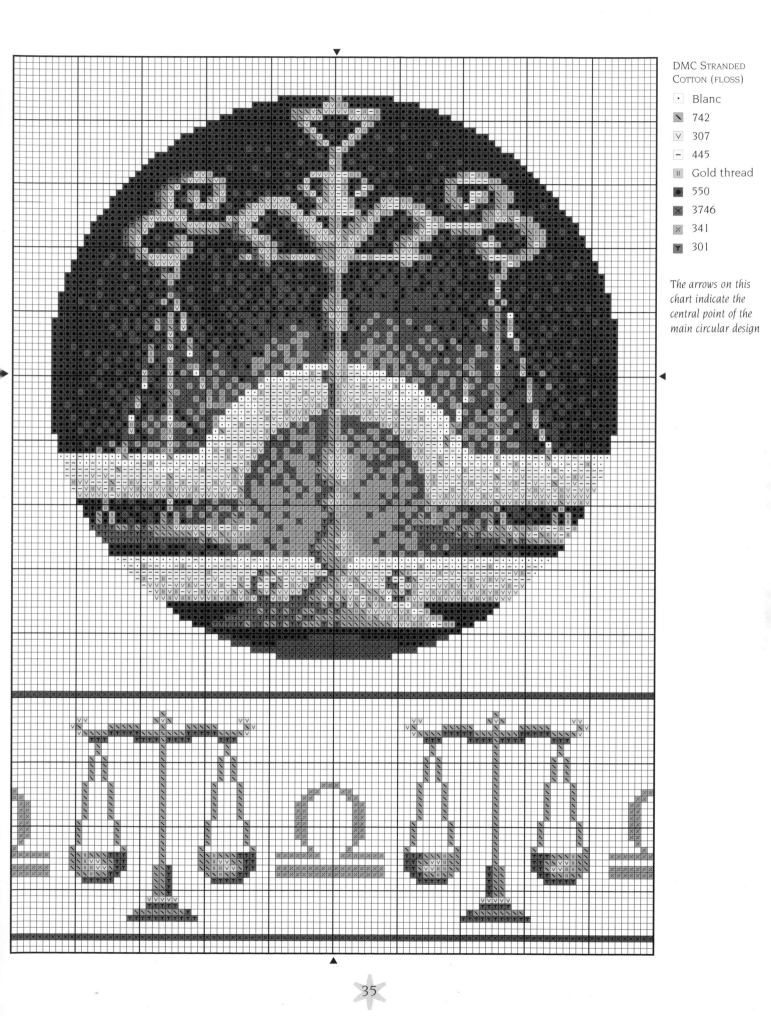

DMC STRANDED
COTTON (FLOSS)

· Blanc
◺ 742
∨ 307
– 445
‖ Gold thread
● 550
✕ 3746
⁄ 341
⊤ 301

The arrows on this chart indicate the central point of the main circular design

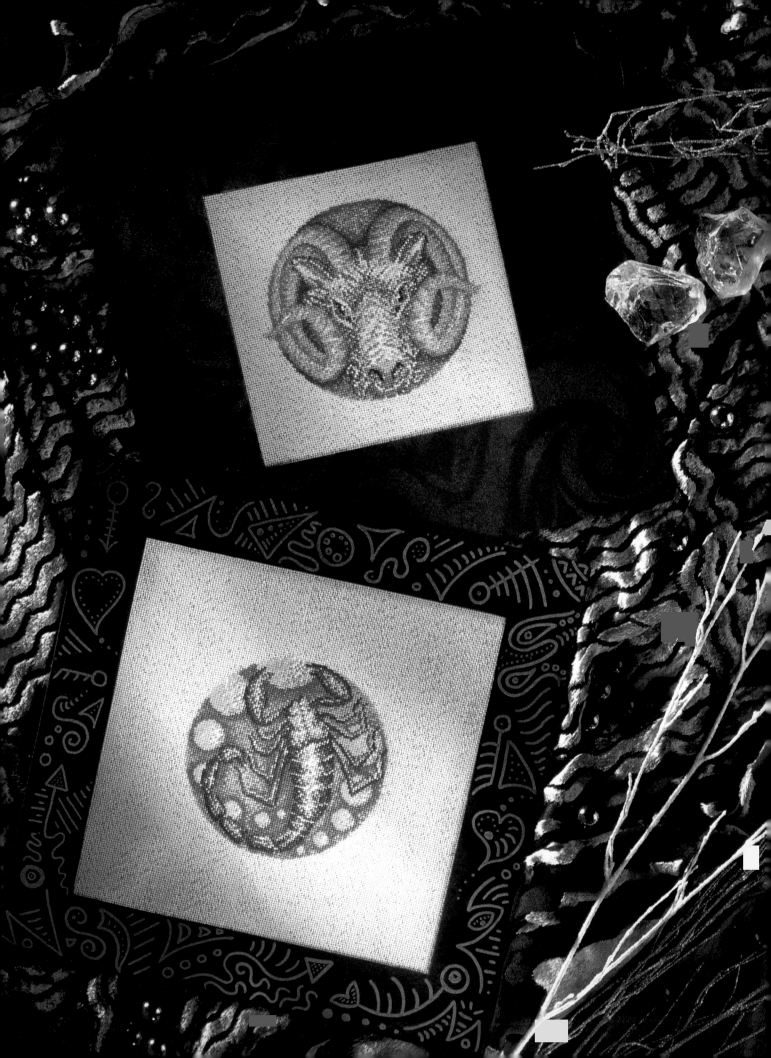

Scorpio the Scorpion

24 October – 22 November

Greek legend tells two stories associated with the sign of Scorpio. First, Scorpio represents the scorpion that stung the handsome, giant hunter, Orion, to death. It is said that is why Orion sets as Scorpio rises. Second, when Phaeton, son of Helios, drove the fiery chariot of the Sun, a scorpion stung the horses, and they bolted. Out of control, the Sun came too near the earth, causing great destruction.

✱ Scorpio's ruling planets are Mars and Pluto. Typical Scorpios are intense, strong-willed and self-confident, often aggressive and stimulated by conflict. A magnetic personality and outstanding powers of leadership give them people's respect rather than affection. Under pressure, they tend to be jealous, resentful, stubborn, obstinate, secretive, rebellious, suspicious and self-indulgent.

Zodiac Decorated Card

On this third hand-decorated card, a simple metallic gold pen is put to great effect. Strikingly sinuous shapes echoing the curves of the scorpion fill the surround, creating a dramatic contrast to the black background.

- ✱ Thick black card, 28 x 56cm (11 x 22in)
- ✱ Contrasting thin card, 26.5cm (10½in) square
- ✱ A sheet of thin card (card is available from art shops or good stationers)
- ✱ A metallic gold pen (from art shops and crafts suppliers)
- ✱ Scalpel or craft knife
- ✱ Double-sided adhesive tape
- ✱ Craft adhesive
- ✱ Gold fleck Bellana fabric, 20-count, 24cm (9½in) square
- ✱ Medium-weight iron-on interfacing
- ✱ DMC stranded cotton (floss) in the colours listed on the chart
- ✱ DMC fil or clair light gold thread
- ✱ Tapestry needle, No 26

1 Prepare your fabric, find the starting point (see page 10) then, following the chart opposite, work the design downwards. Use one strand of stranded cotton (floss), and the fil or clair gold thread straight from the reel.

2 Press the finished embroidery face down on a soft cloth or towel (see page 122). Then, iron the interfacing on to the wrong side.

3 Make a fold-line dividing the thick black card into two equal sections by measuring 28cm (11in) along the width and lightly marking a line on the wrong side. Using the scalpel or craft knife, cut an aperture 20.5cm (8in) square from the left-hand section. With the back of the blade, gently score the fold-line previously marked.

4 Draw abstract patterns with the gold metallic pen. If you do not feel confident, sketch patterns on to the card with a soft pencil first. Fold the card in half along the score line. See page 20 for mounting embroidery into a card.

Photographed on page 36–37: the Aries, Libra and Scorpio Decorated Cards. Porcelain trinket boxes are excellent mounts for astrological signs and images. Here, Libra from the zodiac border on page 35 is embroidered on 20-count gold fleck Bellana fabric using one strand of stranded cotton (floss), and set in the lid of a 7.5cm (3in) dark blue porcelain trinket box. To assemble the trinket box lid, see 'Displaying Your Work' on page 123. Also pictured is the image of Scorpio, from the zodiac border on page 39, set in a Framecraft handbag mirror.

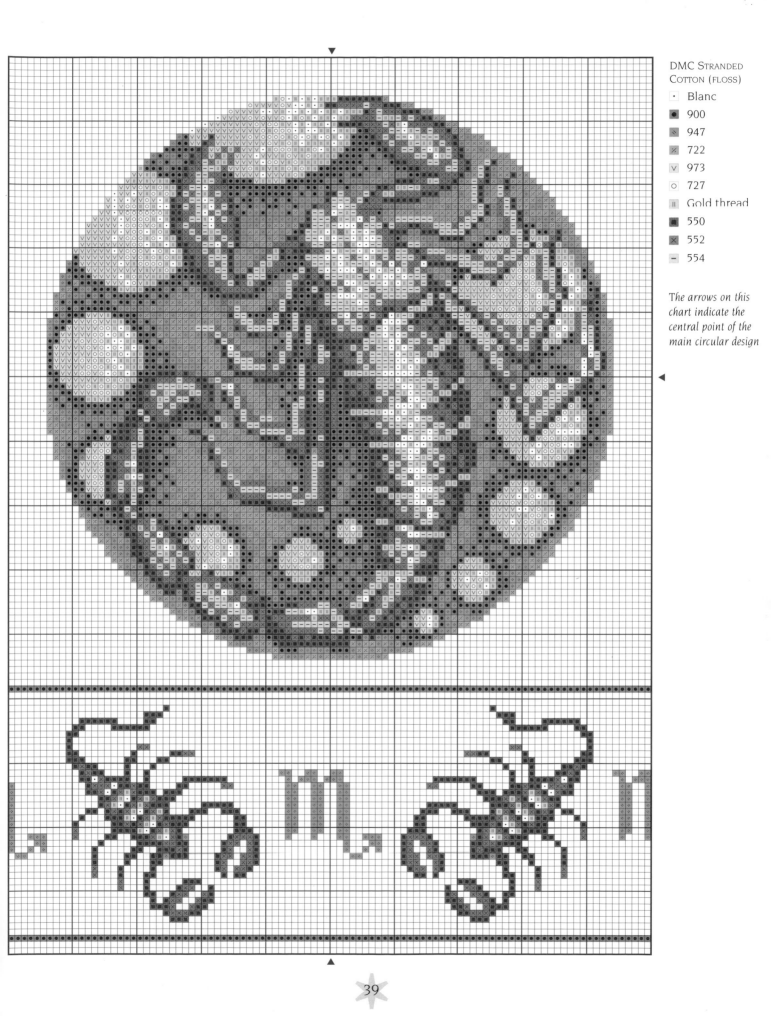

DMC Stranded
Cotton (floss)

- · Blanc
- ● 900
- ◩ 947
- ◪ 722
- ∨ 973
- ○ 727
- ‖ Gold thread
- ▦ 550
- ⨯ 552
- − 554

The arrows on this chart indicate the central point of the main circular design

Sagittarius the Archer

23 November – 21 December

Centaurs, half-men and half-horses, were descended from Centaurus, a son of Apollo. The wisest and best of the Centaurs was Chiron who, skilled in music, medicine, prophecy, hunting and gymnastics, taught many of the heroes of antiquity. When he was accidentally killed by Herakles, Chiron's image was placed amongst the stars as Sagittarius by Zeus.

✱ Sagittarius' ruling planet is Jupiter. The Sagittarian personality is honest, open, optimistic, loyal and independent. Generous and outgoing, Sagittarians like to be surrounded by friends, and often spend money impulsively. Under pressure, they tend to be self-indulgent, conceited and tactless.

Zodiac Clothing

Personalising clothing with a birth sign makes a really unusual gift for someone special. With the help of waste canvas you can apply a design to any fabric. This special canvas, loosely woven, stiffened and held together by water-soluble glue, comes in a number of thread counts, and often contains a thread of a different colour, woven through at regular intervals to help your counting and to ensure the canvas aligns with the base fabric.

✱ An item of clothing of your choice
✱ Waste canvas, 14-count, 23cm (9in) square
✱ Tacking (basting) thread
✱ DMC stranded cotton (floss) in colours listed on chart
✱ DMC fil or clair gold thread
✱ Tapestry needle, No 24
✱ Pair of fine tweezers
✱ Spray-bottle of water

1 Determine the finished size of your design and cut out a piece of waste canvas about 4cm (1½in) wider and deeper than the motif.

2 Align the coloured threads in the waste canvas with the weave of the fabric on which you are stitching the design. Alternatively, align the waste canvas with a seam of the garment. Pin then tack (baste) the waste canvas into position.

3 Treat each pair of canvas threads as a single thread, and stitch the design as you would over any evenweave fabric. Begin from the top and work downwards, using the required number of strands: for example – two strands for cross stitch and one for backstitch on 14-count.

4 Start and finish off the threads in the normal way: by anchoring the starting thread under the first few stitches and by threading the finished ends back under four or five stitches. If you are adding the motif to a garment that will be washed often, you may want to begin and end threads in a small knot for extra security.

5 When you have completed the embroidery, cut away the excess canvas, leaving about 1.2cm (½in) all round.

6 Lightly spray the embroidery with warm water. Use fine tweezers to pull out the canvas threads one by one. Resist the temptation to pull out more than one at a time – if you do, you may damage your embroidery. You may have to re-dampen your work from time to time.

7 Place the finished piece right-side down on a soft, dry towel and press it lightly.

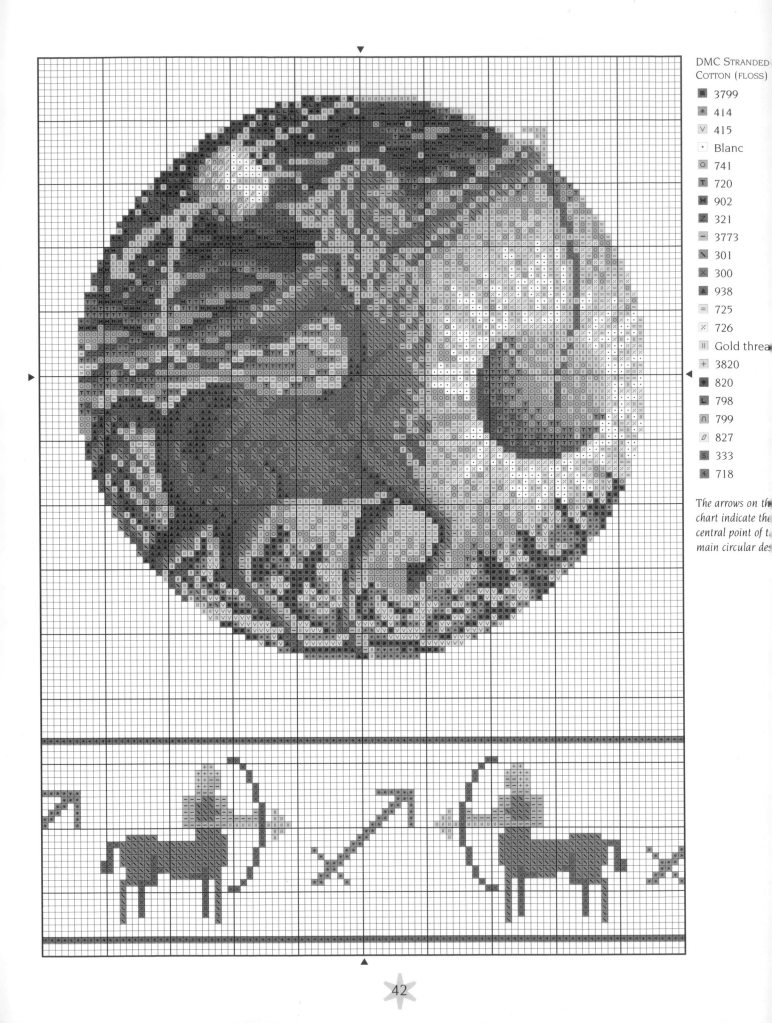

DMC STRANDED COTTON (FLOSS)

- ◼ 3799
- ✳ 414
- ⋁ 415
- ∙ Blanc
- ⊙ 741
- T 720
- ◰ 902
- ◪ 321
- ▬ 3773
- ◥ 301
- ⊠ 300
- ▲ 938
- = 725
- ⫽ 726
- ‖ Gold thread
- ✛ 3820
- ✳ 820
- L 798
- ∩ 799
- ⧄ 827
- ▨ 333
- ⧆ 718

The arrows on the chart indicate the central point of the main circular design

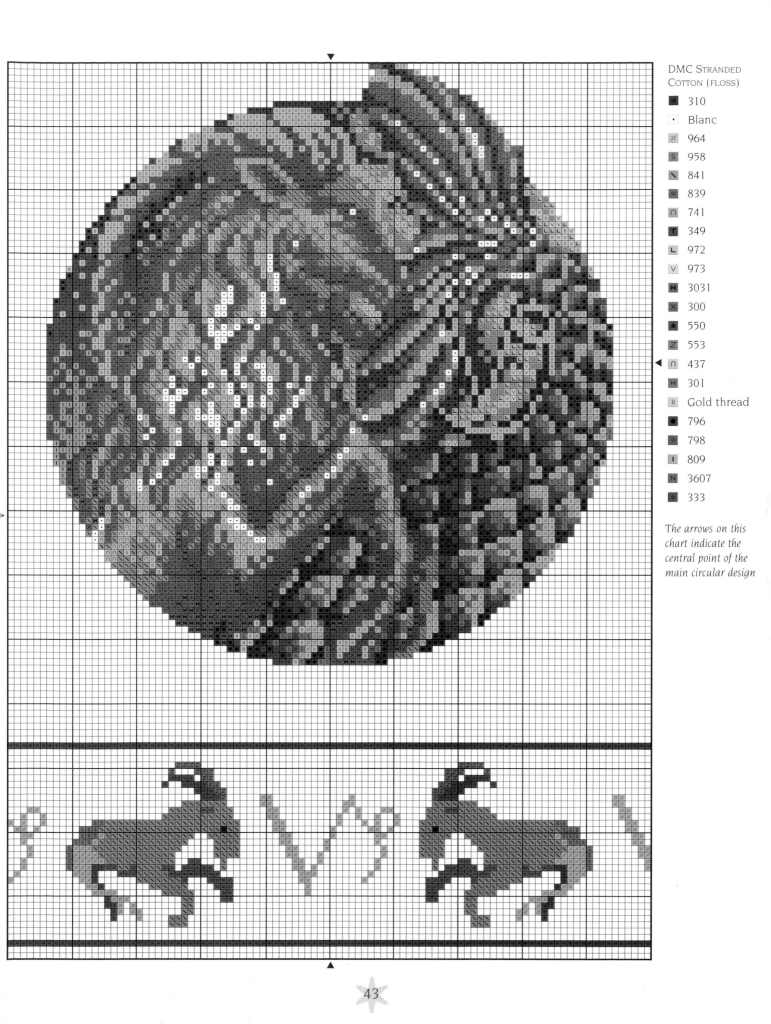

DMC STRANDED
COTTON (FLOSS)

■	310
·	Blanc
⁒	964
S	958
◥	841
▤	839
∩	741
T	349
L	972
V	973
⋈	3031
✗	300
★	550
Z	553
∩	437
H	301
‖	Gold thread
◆	796
◥	798
I	809
N	3607
▨	333

The arrows on this chart indicate the central point of the main circular design

Capricorn the Goat-fish

22 December – 20 January

Capricorn's strange goat-fish body might be explained by the story of the god Pan who, as he was changing into animal shape, jumped into the water to avoid the monster Typhon. The half of Pan above the water turned into goat; the half below became fish. According to another Greek myth, however, the goat Amalthea acted as nurse to baby Zeus. Her reward was to be placed amongst the stars as Capricorn.

✱ Capricorn's ruling planet is Saturn. Capricorns take life seriously. They are by nature ambitious, cautious, honest, efficient and industrious. They do not rush into friendships, but are fiercely loyal. Under pressure, Capricorns tend to be secretive, mean, pessimistic, rigid, stubborn, egotistical and demanding.

ZODIAC HAND-DECORATED JEWELLED FRAME

This striking jewelled frame is easy to make, and enhances the design by picking out jewels that match colours in the actual embroidery.

✱ Black Aida fabric, 14-count, 35.5cm (14in) square
✱ DMC stranded cotton (floss) in the colours listed on the chart
✱ DMC fil or clair light gold thread
✱ Tapestry needle, No 24
✱ Firm mounting board, 25.5 cm (10in) square
✱ Masking tape
✱ A picture frame of your choice
✱ Craft adhesive
✱ A tube of gold relief outliner available from art shops and good crafts suppliers (usually used in glass painting)
✱ Jewellery stones of your choice available from crafts suppliers

1 Prepare your fabric, find the starting point (see page 10) then, following the Capricorn chart on page 43, work the design downwards. Use two strands of stranded cotton (floss), and the fil or clair gold thread, which is not stranded, straight from the reel.

2 When you have completed the embroidery, place it face down on a soft cloth or towel and press it carefully (see page 122).

3 See 'Mounting embroideries for framing' on page 122 to mount and frame the finished embroidery.

4 Place the framed picture on a firm, flat surface, and position your chosen jewellery stones to the best effect. When you are happy with the effect, glue them into place using the craft adhesive. Put to one side, and leave to dry.

5 Next, carefully outline each jewellery stone with the gold relief outliner (see page 9). Leave to dry.

This grouping of projects worked from the Capricorn chart on page 43 shows how versatile the zodiac charts can be. The main design has been worked as a framed picture; the border design has been repeated to create a shelf border, embroidered on to a 12cm (4½in) woven edge Aida band using a single strand of stranded cotton; and single elements of the border design have been worked on 18-count Aida fabric and set in an oval porcelain trinket box and a round miniature brass frame.

Sun and Moon

Throughout the ages, both sun and moon have been worshipped by peoples across the world. Most powerful was probably the sun, the giver of life. For the ancient Egyptians, this was the god Ra sailing across the sky each day, disappearing into the Underworld at night. The Greek sun was Helios, driving a flaming chariot through the heavens. Ancient kings and queens believed themselves brothers, sisters and children of the sun.

✶ In contrast, the moon was the embodiment of motherhood. As the new moon she was the goddess of birth and growth; at full moon she became the goddess of love and war; and as the old moon she was the goddess of death and divination.

CELESTIAL MIRROR

Traditional sun and moon symbols shine brightly around this glorious mirror resplendent with celestial imagery. Although the mirror would be exquisite in any setting, its mystical theme is particularly appropriate for a bedroom.

✶ Navy Aida fabric, 18-count, 46cm (18in) square
✶ DMC stranded cotton (floss) in the colours listed on the chart
✶ Tapestry needle, No 26
✶ Mounting board, 38 x 36.5cm (15 x 14½ in)
✶ Mirror cut to the same size as the mounting board
✶ Masking tape
✶ Scalpel or craft knife
✶ Double-sided adhesive tape
✶ A picture frame of your choice

1 Prepare your fabric, find the starting point (see page 10) then, following the chart on pages 48 and 49, work the design downwards. Use two strands of stranded cotton (floss).

2 When you have completed the embroidery, press, following the instructions on page 122.

3 From the mounting board, carefully cut out a central window measuring 13.5 x 12cm (5¼ x 4¾ in). Place your embroidery face down on a firm, flat surface and position the mounting board on top of it ensuring it is positioned accurately.

4 Next, mark the cut-out on the fabric with a soft pencil. Using a sharp pair of scissors, make a small nick in the centre of the fabric, and cut diagonally from the centre out to each marked corner. Place the mounting board over the fabric again, and fold the triangles of fabric to the back of the board, securing them with masking tape. Next, fold in the outer edges of fabric, mitring the corners and securing them with tape.

5 Fix your mirror into position with the double-sided tape. See 'Mounting embroideries for framing' on page 122 to mount and frame your finished embroidery.

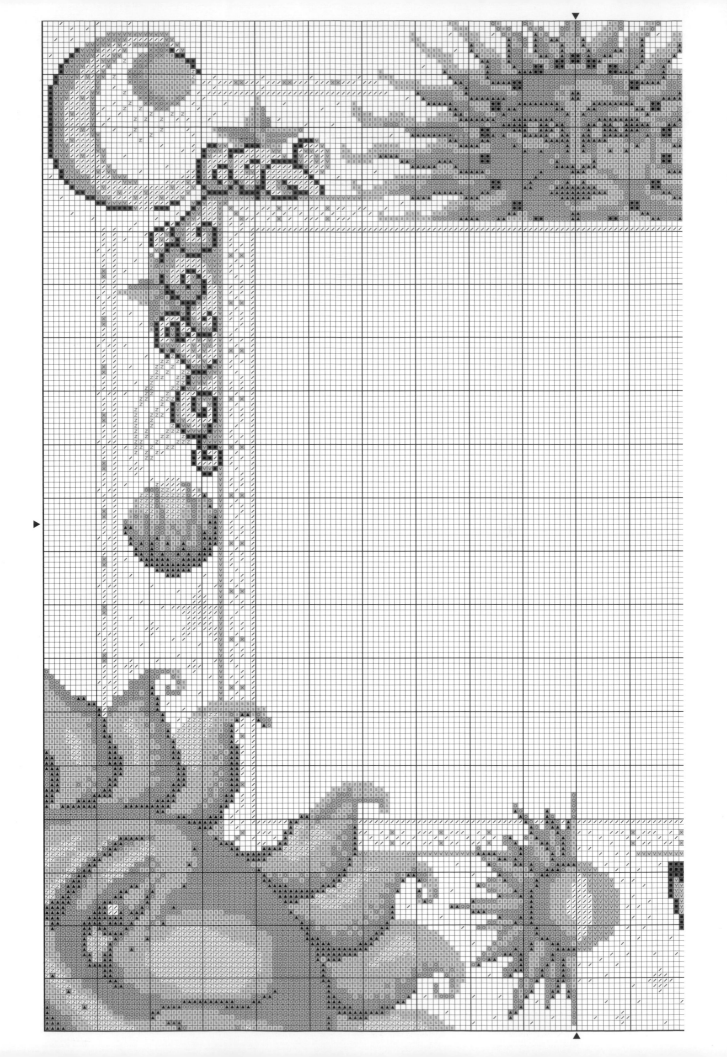

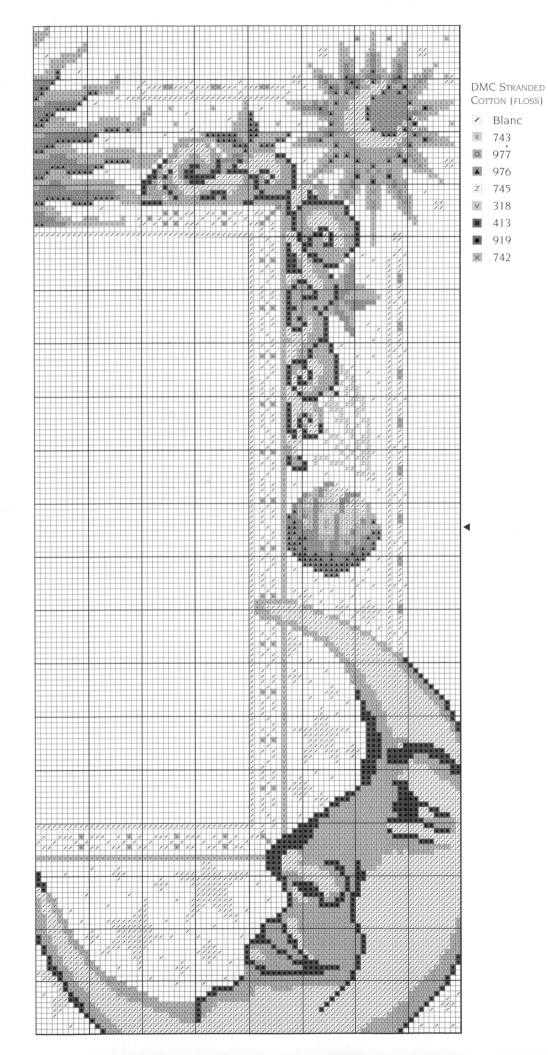

DMC STRANDED
COTTON (FLOSS)

✓	Blanc
II	743
O	977
▲	976
z	745
V	318
■	413
●	919
✕	742

The Planets

The ancients thought that the planets were stars that wandered through the heavens. These celestial movements through the skies were used to interpret the events and nature of man's life. Astrologically, the planets (including the sun and moon, known as the Greater and Lesser Lights) each have their own personality which affects people in different ways. The zodiac signs are also endowed with specific characteristics as they are each ruled by a particular planet.

✱ Briefly, the Lights and planets have the following attributes: Sun – power and creativity; Moon – emotion and nurturing; Uranus – change and unpredictability; Neptune – intuition and mysticism; Jupiter – benevolence and maturity; Mars – energy and passion; Venus – harmony and warmth; Mercury – communications and activity; Pluto – elimination and regeneration; Saturn – limitation and control.

PLANETS NIGHTDRESS CASE

Make this luxurious padded case to tuck away your nightie or pyjamas during the day. With the combination of bright colours and gold thread on the black fabric, it will look beautiful sitting on top of any bed.

- ✱ Black Aida fabric, 14-count, 95 x 48.5cm (37½ x 19in)
- ✱ Lightweight polyester batting (wadding), 95 x 48.5cm (37½ x 19in)
- ✱ Contrasting lightweight cotton fabric for the lining, 95 x 48.5cm (37½ x 19in)
- ✱ DMC stranded cotton (floss) in the colours listed on the chart
- ✱ DMC fil or clair light gold thread
- ✱ Tapestry needle, No 24
- ✱ Matching sewing thread

All the measurements given above include a 1.5cm (⅝ in) seam allowance.
Final size of nightdress case – 30.5 x 46cm (12 x 18in)

1 Prepare your fabric (see page 10). Find the starting point by measuring 1.5cm (⅝in) in from the centre of the bottom, short side of the fabric. Then, following the Planets chart on pages 52 and 53, work the design upwards across the width. Use two strands of stranded cotton (floss), and the fil or clair gold thread, which is not stranded, straight from the reel.

2 When you have completed the embroidery, place it face down on a soft cloth or towel and press it carefully (see page 122).

3 Place your embroidered fabric face down on a firm, flat surface, and carefully smooth the batting (wadding) on top. Pin and tack (baste) these together. Trim the batting (wadding) back almost to the tacking (basting) line (seam allowance line), and catch-stitch around the edge. Remove the pins and tacking (basting) stitches.

4 Make a single 1.5cm (⅝in) turning across the width (not the flap edge) of the fabric and tack (baste). With right sides facing, fold the pocket front section over for 30cm (11¾in); tack (baste), and machine stitch to form the pocket. Clip excess fabric from the corners, remove tacking (basting) and turn right side out.

5 Make a single turning on the short edge of the lining fabric and repeat as for the embroidered Aida fabric, but do not turn the pocket to the right side.

6 With the right sides of the Aida fabric and the lining together, tack (baste) and machine stitch around the flap, finishing just above the side seams. Trim away the excess fabric from the corners and turn the flap through to the right side. Slip the lightweight, cotton lining fabric into the pocket section and slipstitch the two top edges together, easing the turning so that the stitching is on the inside. Remove the tacking (basting) stitches.

THE RULING PLANETS OF THE ZODIAC SIGNS:

AQUARIUS	Uranus and Saturn	**CANCER**	Moon
		LEO	Sun
PISCES	Neptune and Jupiter	**VIRGO**	Mercury
		LIBRA	Venus
ARIES	Mars	**SCORPIO**	Mars and Pluto
TAURUS	Venus	**SAGITTARIUS**	Jupiter
GEMINI	Mercury	**CAPRICORN**	Saturn

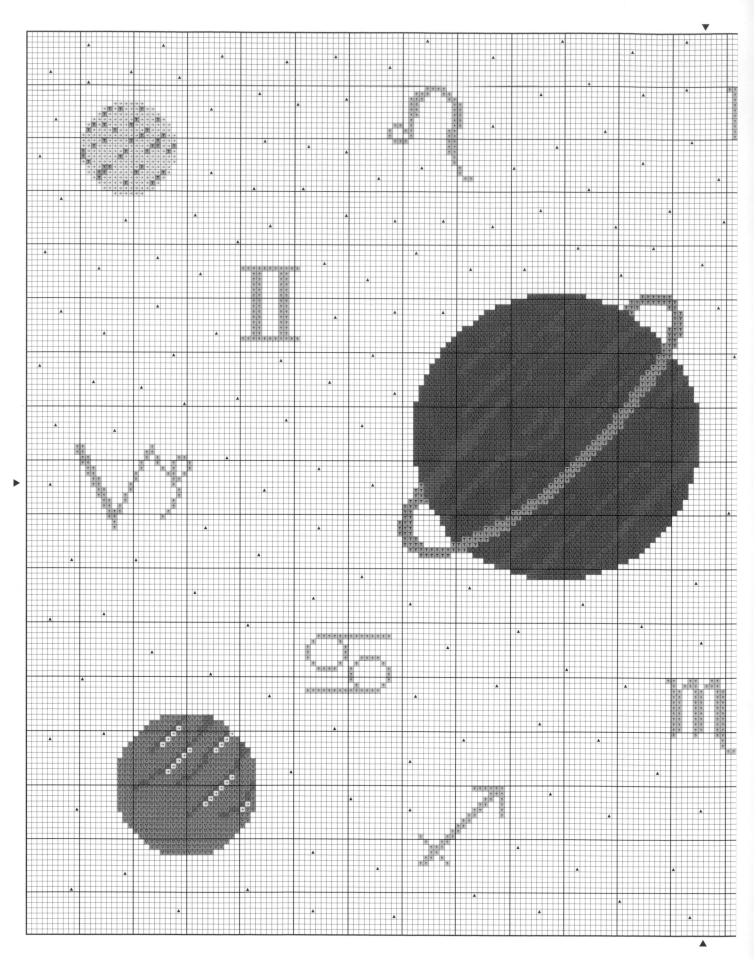

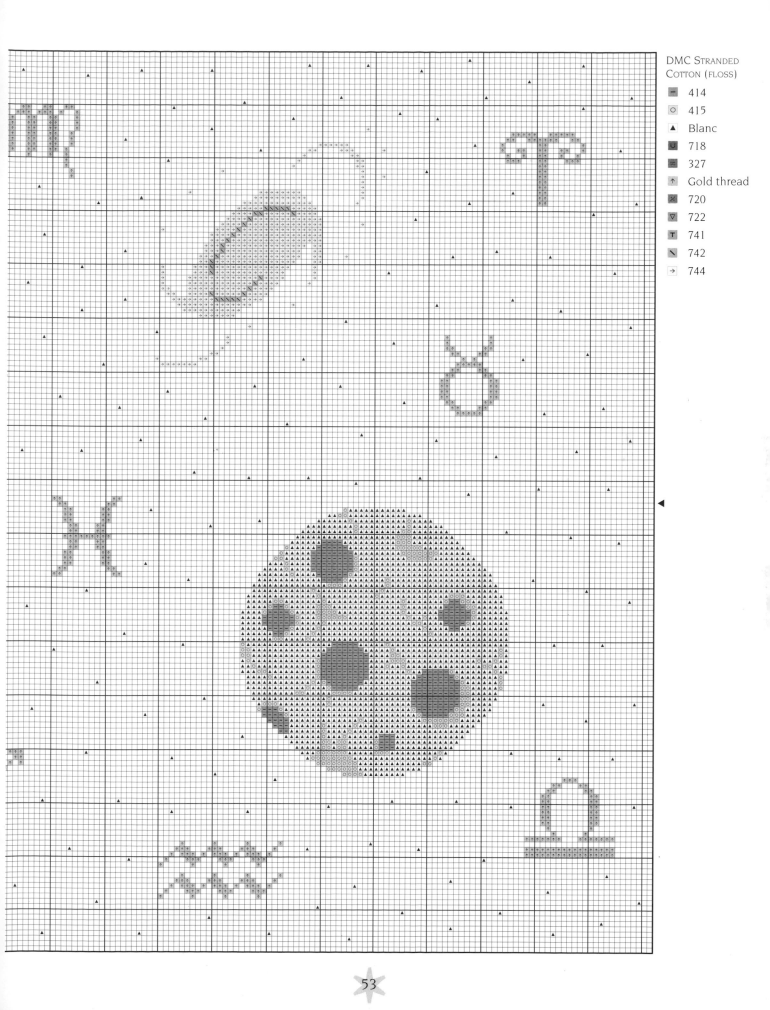

DMC STRANDED
COTTON (FLOSS)

⚊	414
○	415
▲	Blanc
Ⅱ	718
▨	327
↑	Gold thread
▨	720
▽	722
T	741
╲	742
→	744

Mythical Beasts

*O*ver the centuries, man has devised a menagerie of curious and fanciful imaginary creatures. Frequently presentations of nightmarish fears and imaginative ideas, these supernatural figures have found a permanent place in the world of mythology and legend.

It was once believed that every phenomenon of water, sky and air was the work of various monsters, spirits or deities, rewarding or punishing mankind for his actions. These spirits, it was thought, interfere with the affairs of men, and hold mankind at their mercy.

As in the human community, these spirits range in temperament from pernicious to magnanimous and from tyrants to minor officials. They may be destructive, helpful, mischievous, or erratic: directors of the elements or nothing more than tormentors of mankind.

This section brings together a wide selection of mythical beasts from fantasy, ancient mythology and heraldry: the unicorn, Pegasus, an oriental dragon, Egyptian deities Thoth and Anubis, and heraldic beasts the pantheon and the sea-horse.

Unicorn

Unicorns were believed to be powerful and wondrous steeds, with glistening coats of pure white, piercing eyes, and a single sharp, twisted horn, two to three feet in length, growing from the centre of their forehead; its powerful properties protected unicorns from being possessed by magic. Anyone who drank from a unicorn's horn was thought to be protected from stomach trouble, epilepsy and poison.

★ Unicorns were ferocious but good creatures who avoided contact with all but the woodland spirits. They did not live in herds but made their home in an open dell of the forest they chose to protect. Occasionally they permitted themselves to be ridden by a virgin or elf maiden of pure heart. If treated kindly, the unicorn would be her steed for life, even carrying her far beyond the realm of his forest if she so wished, and protecting her until her death. Unicorns lived for over 1000 years, maintaining their youth until death was only weeks away. The secret to this longevity was in the strong magical power of the horn.

Pegasus and Unicorn Cushions

To make this pair of cushions, follow the instructions on page 60 using the materials listed below. The chart for Pegasus is on pages 62 and 63, and the chart for the unicorn is on pages 58 and 59.

For each 35.5cm (14in) square cushion, you will need:
★ Navy Zweigart Aida fabric, 18-count, 38cm (15in) square
★ Contrasting backing fabric 38cm (15in) square
★ A cushion pad, 35.5cm (14in) square
★ DMC stranded embroidery cotton (floss) in the colours listed on the chart
★ Sewing thread to match fabric
★ Tapestry needle, No 26
★ Contrasting 6mm cord, 1.5m (59in)

All measurements include a 1.5cm (⅝in) seam allowance.

Alternative Projects

Quick to work, these Pegasus and Unicorn small projects make lovely gifts. Choose individual images from the border charts on page 61 and mount them in a range of settings, such as:

Silver plated miniature frame – the Pegasus head on 18-count Aida fabric using two strands of stranded cotton (floss), set in a Framecraft 9cm (3⅜in) round silver plated miniature frame;

Frosted glass bowl – the Pegasus head on navy 18-count Aida fabric using two strands of stranded cotton (floss), set in the lid of a 9cm (3in) round frosted glass bowl;

Notelet holder – a pair of Pegasus heads on an 8.5cm (3 ½in) woven-edge Aida band, using one strand of stranded cotton (floss);

Dressing table mirror – the Unicorn head on 22-count Christmas red Hardanger fabric, using a single strand of stranded cotton (floss);

Wooden trinket box – the Unicorn head on 22-count Hardanger fabric using one strand of stranded cotton (floss), mounted on the lid of a wooden trinket box from Mac Gregor Designs.

Unicorns:

★ could sense an enemy from a great distance
★ moved silently, and ran faster than any other creature of the forest
★ attacked anyone found killing for sport or damaging the forest

DMC STRANDED
COTTON (FLOSS)

‖	414
⁄	415
·	Blanc
■	310
×	743
s	976
✕	919
○	745
T	977

Pegasus

Pegasus, the magnificent immortal winged horse from Greek mythology, was dedicated to serving the powers of goodness and light. Very shy, wild and not easily tamed, he only allowed good characters to become his master. Once chosen, he served them with absolute faithfulness for the rest of their lives. Yet his mother was the evil, snake-haired monster, Medusa who could turn you to stone with but a glance.

✱ The famous hero Bellepheron rode Pegasus on many amazing adventures, but overreached himself when he tried to ride up Mount Olympus to the very home of the gods. Such presumption angered Zeus, and he sent a gadfly to sting Pegasus. Bellepheron was thrown to Earth, and was so badly injured that he was never to regain his prowess. Pegasus, however, arrived at the top of Mount Olympus and, from that day on, carried Zeus' thunderbolts and lightning.

PEGASUS AND UNICORN CUSHIONS

The glory of these wonderful mythical horses has been captured in two fabulous designs: Pegasus flying through the sparkling night sky, lit only by the protecting moon; the unicorn striding through the early morning mist, greeting the newly risen sun. To work them as a stunning pair of cushions, follow the instructions below, using the list of materials on page 56.

1 Prepare your fabric, find the starting point (see page 10) then, following the Pegasus chart on pages 62 and 63 or the Unicorn chart on pages 58 and 59, work the design downwards. Use two strands of stranded cotton (floss).

2 When you have completed the embroidery, place it face down on a soft cloth or towel and press it carefully (see page 122).

3 Place your embroidery right side up on a firm, flat surface, placing the backing fabric on top of the embroidered square, right sides together. Pin and tack (baste) three sides of the cushion.

4 Machine-stitch the tacked (basted) seams and then clip excess fabric from the corners. Remove the pins and tacking (basting) stitches, and turn to the right side.

5 Press in the seam allowance along each side of the opening. Place the cushion pad inside the cover, and oversew the edges together. Using small catch stitches, stitch the contrasting cord all round the cushion along the seam line.

PEGASUS:

✱ would not accept a saddle, so was always ridden bareback
✱ spoke his own language, but could communicate with horses, and understand all languages
✱ in combat, attacked with his hooves as well as his teeth, and was able to dive upon an enemy from heights of more than fifty feet
✱ was extremely intelligent, and had the gift of detecting good and evil in the human heart; would not hesitate to throw from his back any evil person attempting to tame him.

Pegasus

DMC STRANDED
COTTON (FLOSS)

- ▦ 414
- ◪ 415
- ○ Blanc
- T 727
- ▼ 725
- ✳ 310

Unicorn

DMC STRANDED
COTTON (FLOSS)

- ▦ 414
- ◪ 415
- · Blanc
- ■ 310
- ✕ 743
- T 977

DMC Stranded
Cotton (floss)

⊞ 414

⟋ 415

○ Blanc

T 727

▼ 725

✳ 310

Oriental Dragon

Water-spirits of the clouds and seas, oriental dragons were also associated with the moon. It was said that the dragon's waking, sleeping and breathing determined night and day, the season, rainfall and wind. Unlike ferocious European dragons, Chinese dragons brought – and still bring – good luck. In New Year's Day parades people wind through the streets in dragon costumes to prevent evil spirits spoiling the New Year.

✱ There were five types of dragon: heavenly - guarding gods; imperial – guarding emperors; spiritual – controlling wind and rain; earthly – deepening rivers and seas; and guardians of hidden treasure.

ORIENTAL DRAGON WALL HANGING

The oriental dragon from pages 66, 67 and 68 has been made up into an eye-catching wall hanging, decorated with an assortment of plain and beaded tassels to compliment the fabric and silks used for the embroidery. In addition to this stylised design, three traditional designs from ancient Chinese symbolism are provided on the chart. They represent (from the top): double joy which signifies married happiness; longevity; and finally, the symbol for dragon.

✱ Mahogany finish 2.5cm (1in) curtain pole, 63.5cm (25in)

✱ Black Aida fabric, 14-count, 70 x 43cm (27½ x 17in)

✱ Black lightweight cotton backing fabric, 70 x 43cm (27½ x 17in)

✱ DMC stranded cotton (floss) in the colours listed on the chart

✱ Matching sewing thread

✱ Tapestry needle, No 24

✱ Black 5mm cord, 1m (39½in)

✱ Nineteen tassels

All measurements include a 1.5cm (⅝ in) seam allowance.

1 Prepare your fabric (see page 10) and find your starting point, in the centre, 14cm (5½in) down from the top edge. Then, following the chart on pages 66, 67 and 68, work the design downwards. Use two strands of stranded cotton (floss) for cross stitch, and one for backstitch.

2 When you have completed the embroidery, place it face down on a soft cloth or towel and press it carefully (see page 122).

3 Cut a curve at the bottom edge of the Aida, beginning approximately 9cm (3½in) up from each side edge. Cut backing to the same shape.

4 Place the embroidered fabric face up on a firm, flat surface, and place the backing on top, right sides facing. Pin and tack (baste) together along the long edges and curve.

5 Machine stitch the long edges and round the curve, leaving the short edge open for turning. Remove tacking (basting) stitches.

6 Press the seams open, turn to the right side and press. Turn in the seam allowance on the top edge, and slip stitch together. Turn over a 5cm (2in) hem at the top and slip stitch in place, making a casement for the curtain pole.

7 Stitch the tassels in place by hand on the back of the hanging along the curve, ensuring that they are evenly spaced. Stitch the cord into place round the curtain pole for hanging.

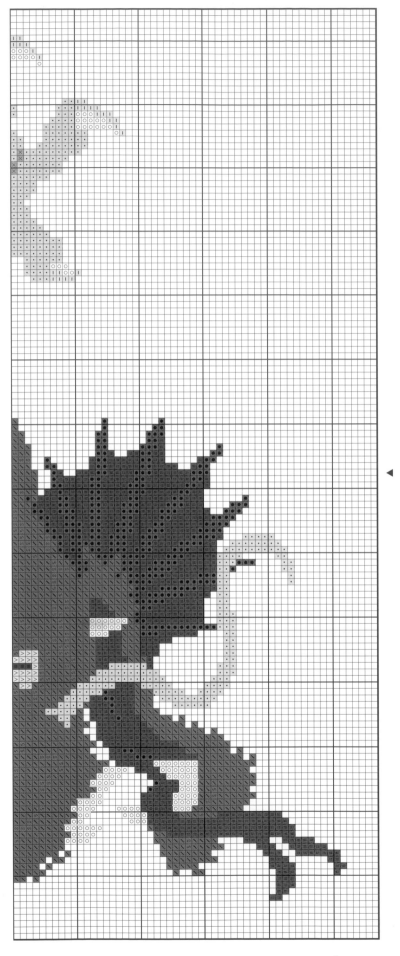

DMC STRANDED
COTTON (FLOSS)

- 415
○ Blanc
▦ 666
● 816
▨ 910
▣ 3818
· 3821
✕ 783
∨ 307
▦ 310
  Backstitch outline:
▨ 318

Opposite

Symbols from the oriental dragon chart on page 66 are featured here in DMC greetings card blanks. The dragon symbol is stitched on red 22-count Hardanger fabric using one strand of stranded cotton (floss), while the longevity symbol is stitched on navy 18-count Aida fabric using two strands of stranded cotton (floss). The double joy symbol is stitched on navy 14-count Aida fabric using two strands of stranded cotton (floss), and mounted in a 5.5cm (2⅛in) round paperweight. For making up instructions, see 'Displaying Your Work' on page 122. As a special gift for an avid bookworm, why not embroider all three symbols on to a Framecraft bookmark?

Egyptian Mythology

The remarkable pantheon that ruled the lives of ancient Egyptians was amazingly diverse. As even the smallest town had its own god, there were deities almost beyond number, many taking the shapes of animals. Amongst the most important Egyptian deities were those associated with the afterlife – Osiris, lord of the underworld; Anubis, his jackal-headed son; and Thoth, the ibis-headed divine scribe.

✱ Anubis, patron of embalmers and protector of mummies, was guardian of the underworld, guiding the newly arrived dead to the hall of judgement. He weighed each soul against the feather of truth, and Thoth recorded the result. Thoth was associated with the moon, credited with the invention of hieroglyphics and the foundation of law, and became master of magic arts. 'The Book of Thoth' is a traditional name for tarot cards.

FRAMED PICTURES OF THE GODS

The simple, smooth shapes of hieroglyphics, and the formal imagery of Egyptian art translate extremely effectively into cross stitch. Rather than blended shades, blocks of jewel-like solid colour mirror the rich decoration that was an integral part of ancient Egyptian life. Walls of public buildings and burial chambers were densely covered; which makes it particularly appropriate to frame Egyptian figures – such as my re-creation of Thoth and Anubis – as pictures to decorate the walls of a modern home.

For each picture you will need:

* ✳ Natural Floba fabric, 18-count, 33 x 25.5cm (13 x 10 in)
* ✳ DMC stranded cotton (floss) in the colours listed on the chart
* ✳ Tapestry needle, No 26
* ✳ Firm mounting board, 21.5 x 29cm (8½ x 11½ in)
* ✳ Masking tape
* ✳ Picture frame of your choice

1 Prepare your fabric, find the starting point (see page 10) then, following the Thoth chart on page 73 or the Anubis chart on page 74, work the design downwards. Use two strands of stranded cotton (floss), and one strand for the backstitch.

2 When you have completed the embroidery, place it face down on a soft cloth or towel and press it carefully (see page 122).

3 See 'Mounting embroideries for framing' on page 122 to mount and frame the finished embroidery.

Hieroglyphics from the chart on page 74 make an ideal design for a bookmark. The embroidery is stitched onto a 5cm (2in) Aida band using two strands of stranded cotton (floss). The Ankh border design from page 73 is shown here as a notelet holder. The embroidery is stitched on to a 5cm (2in) Aida band using two strands of stranded cotton (floss).

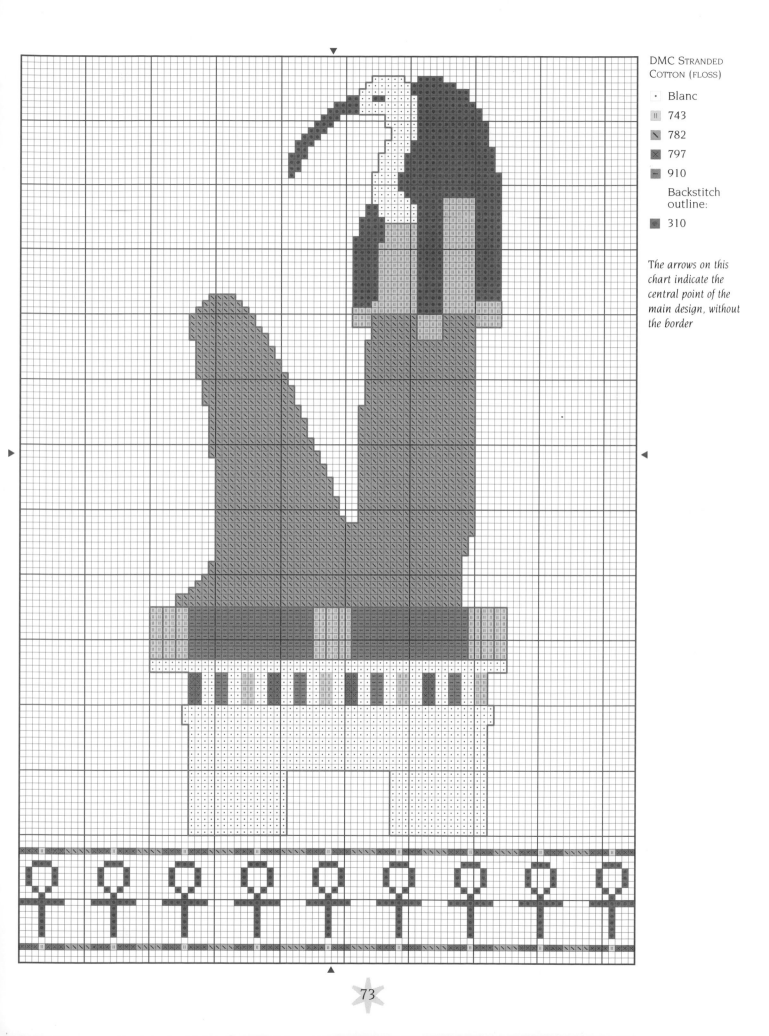

DMC STRANDED
COTTON (FLOSS)

· Blanc

‖ 743

╲ 782

⊠ 797

— 910

Backstitch
outline:

▓ 310

*The arrows on this
chart indicate the
central point of the
main design, without
the border*

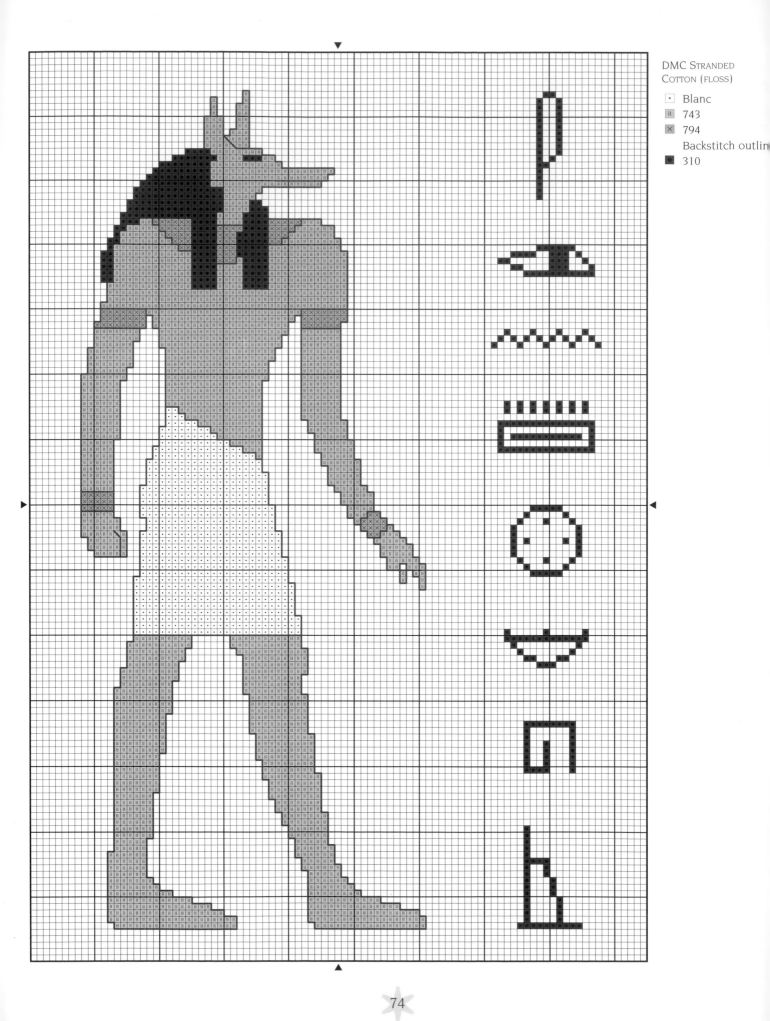

Heraldic Beasts

Colourful, geometric and stylised, heraldic devices have identified their bearers since the early Middle Ages. Originally simple designs carried on shields, they were then applied to textiles and magnificently decorative pennants and badges, saddlecloths and surcoats transformed tournament fields into glittering spectacles. Heraldic emblems were often seen on church needlework, on costume and furnishings. Today, the arms of institutions, colleges and regiments are often worked as pictures, chair seats or cushions.

★ Heraldry describes (or blazons) figures and symbols in a language all of its own. For instance, colours and metals are 'tinctures': gold is or, silver is argent; blue is azure; purple, purpure; green, vert and red, gules. Left is sinister and right is dexter. The Pantheon I've designed (pictured on pages 76/77) could be described as a monster resembling a hind; its tincture purpure, powdered with estoiles or (golden stars).

The crown and fleur-de-lis motifs from the heraldic borders on pages 78 and 79 are shown here embroidered on red 22-count Hardanger fabric using one strand of stranded cotton (floss), and navy 18-count Aida fabric using two strands of stranded cotton (floss), and displayed in a selection of Framecraft porcelain trinket bowls, and a brass pill box. To assemble the lids, see 'Displaying Your Work' on page 122.

*F*RAMED HERALDIC
PICTURES

The Pantheon and Seahorse are exquisite examples of 'supporters', the figures often seen on either side of a shield of arms. Supporters can be birds, beasts, monsters or humans, and are often, as here, exotic fancies, products of a creative imagination. Many outlandish figures are created as hybrids of regular creatures – sea-monsters such as the Seahorse, for example, have the top half of a beast or monster joined to the tail of a fish.

The ancient connection between needlework and heraldry makes it particularly appropriate to feature these intriguing figures as cross stitch pictures.

For each picture you will need:
* Sage Aida fabric, 14-count: 47 x 40.5cm (18½ x 16in) for the Pantheon; 43 x 40.5cm (17 x 16in) for the Seahorse
* DMC stranded cotton (floss) in the colours listed on the chart
* Tapestry needle, No 24
* Firm mounting board: 37 x 30.5cm (14 x 12in) for the Pantheon; 33 x 30.5 (13 x 12in) for the Seahorse
* Masking tape
* Picture frame of your choice

1 Prepare your fabric, find the starting point (see page 10) then, following the Pantheon chart on page 79 or the Seahorse chart on page 78, work the design downwards. Use two strands of stranded cotton (floss), and one strand for the backstitch.

2 When you have completed the embroidery, place it face down on a soft cloth or towel and press it carefully (see page 122).

3 See 'Mounting embroideries for framing' on page 122 to mount and frame the finished embroidery.

The Seahorse picture is shown on the left and the Pantheon creature on the right.

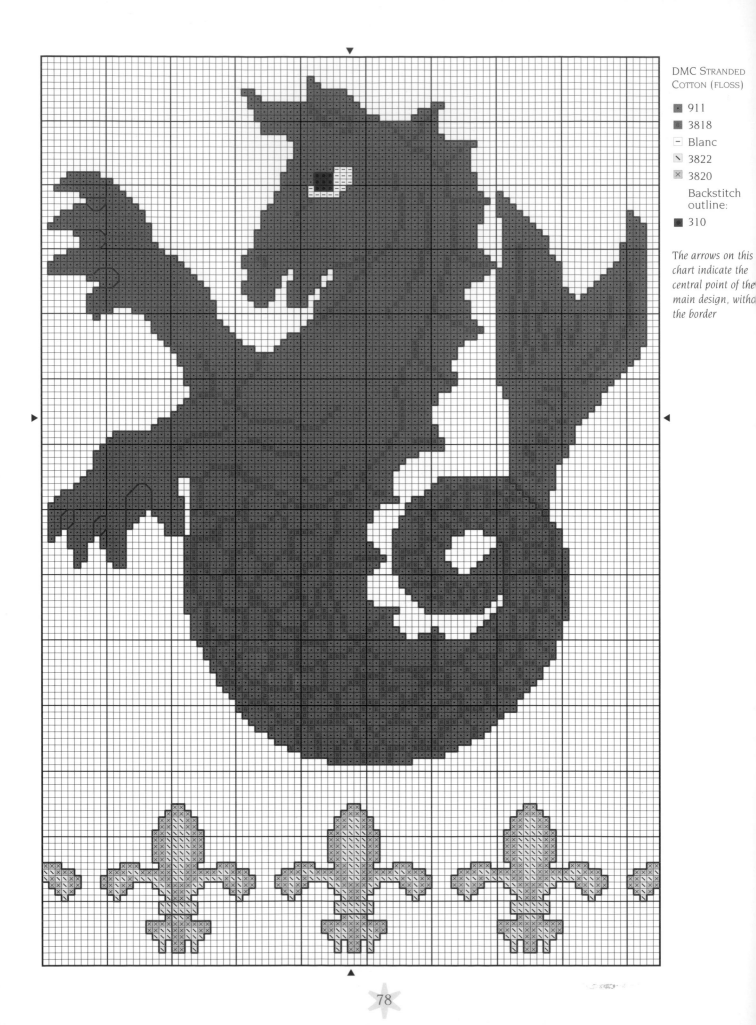

DMC Stranded
Cotton (floss)

■ 911
▥ 3818
⊟ Blanc
◥ 3822
⊠ 3820
Backstitch
outline:
■ 310

The arrows on this
chart indicate the
central point of the
main design, without
the border

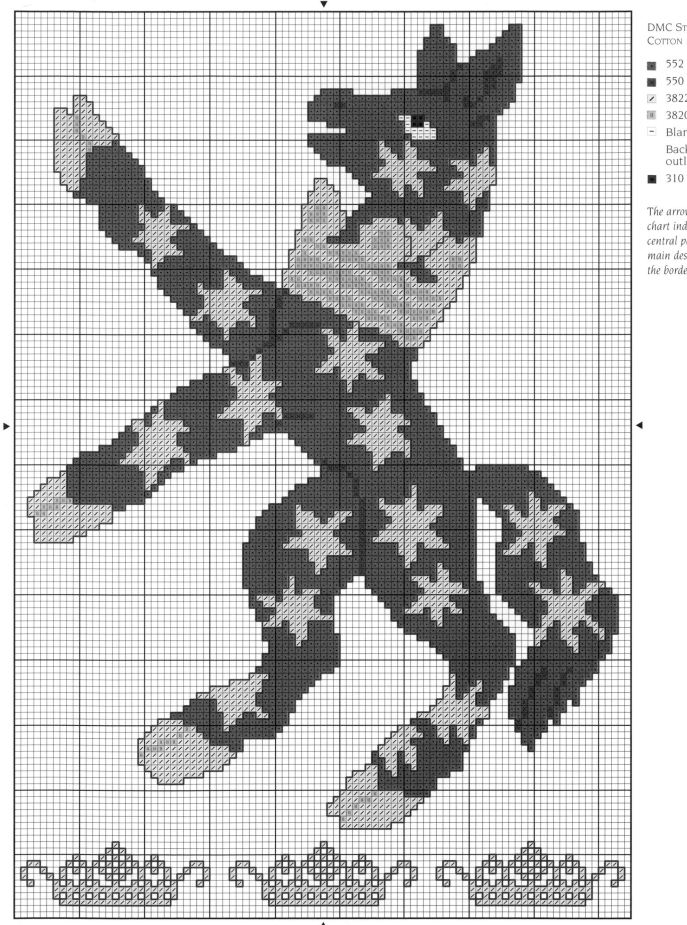

DMC Stranded
Cotton (floss)

- 552
- 550
- 3822
- 3820
- Blanc
  Backstitch
  outline:
- 310

The arrows on this chart indicate the central point of the main design, without the border

Wizards and Warlocks

*T*hroughout history, man has created myths and legends to explain natural phenomena like thunder and lightning, storms and earthquakes. It was widely believed by cultures all over the world that mysterious powers existed all around them – whether in the forests, jungles, mountains, deserts, prairies, sea or sky – which took the form of human-like creatures, often half-human, half-beast, and existed in a different dimension from our own earthly one. Occasionally, these creatures would reveal themselves to humans with good or evil consequences. Witches, wizards and warlocks were able to summon them to appear, or advise humans on spells and offerings to control or appease them.

Taking design inspiration from many different cultures, this section is devoted to these guardians and helpers of mankind: a magnificent wizard casting a spell, Norse warrior-gods, a wise centaur from Greek mythology, and a beautiful mermaid. Guardians and helpers they may be, but it would be foolish to take them for granted. At a whim they can remove their protection – magicians' spells can be turned to evil; gods can lose interest and forget even their favoured mortals; Centaurs can be wild and savage; and beautiful mermaids can lure the unwary to their deaths. There is always just that frisson of danger.

The Wizard

Wizards belonged to the host of myriad magic workers that included magicians, sorcerers, witches, warlocks and fairies. Unlike some who harnessed evil, wizards usually called upon kindly, charitable spirits to activate their spells. In the human world, they frequently held respected positions, as Merlin did in the court of King Arthur.

✱ Each wizard served a prolonged apprenticeship followed by a life devoted to study and research. His was a lonely existence, enduring the rigid disciplines that enabled him to control the wayward power of magic. A wizard paid a high price for the privilege of wearing his distinguishing pointed cap.

Magical Throw

This mystical throw featuring a wizard casting a spell, surrounded by moon motifs, will add mystery to any room.

- ✱ Navy Aida fabric, 14-count, 73.5cm (29in) square
- ✱ Contrasting backing fabric, 73.5cm (29in) square
- ✱ DMC stranded cotton (floss) in the colours listed on the chart
- ✱ Tapestry needle, No 24
- ✱ Matching sewing thread
- ✱ Gold 3mm cord, 3m (114in)
- ✱ Four gold tassels

1 Prepare your fabric, find the starting point (see page 10) then, following the charts on pages 84 to 89, work the design. You may wish to photocopy and stick together the pieces to make a complete chart before you start. Use two strands of stranded cotton (floss) for the cross stitch and one for the backstitch.

2 When you have completed the embroidery, place it face down on a soft cloth or towel and press it carefully (see page 122).

The Educated Wizard

Becoming a wizard involved extensive learning, reading spell books written in many ancient and unfamiliar languages, such as Cornish, Greek, Hebrew and Old Norse. An apprentice wizard created his own set of spell books from those in his master's library.

3 Place the embroidery right side up on a firm, flat surface with the backing fabric on top, right sides together. Pin and tack (baste) three complete sides, and three quarters of the fourth side of the throw, allowing a 1.5cm (⅝in) seam allowance. Machine-stitch the tacked (basted) seams and then clip excess fabric from the corners. Remove the pins and tacking (basting) stitches, and turn to the right side.

4 Press in the seam allowance along the opening, and oversew the edges together. Stitch the cord all round the throw along the seam line, adding a tassel to each corner.

Bed linen turns into something really special when you appliqué on an embroidered Aida band. This bed linen set was perfectly plain and ordinary until it was transformed by the stars and moon border from the chart on pages 84 to 89. Worked with two strands of stranded cotton (floss) on to a 10cm (4in) scalloped edge Aida band. A pretty quilted spectacles case from Framecraft, worked with two strands of stranded cotton (floss), takes on a mystical appeal when decorated with a motif from the star and moon border from the same chart.

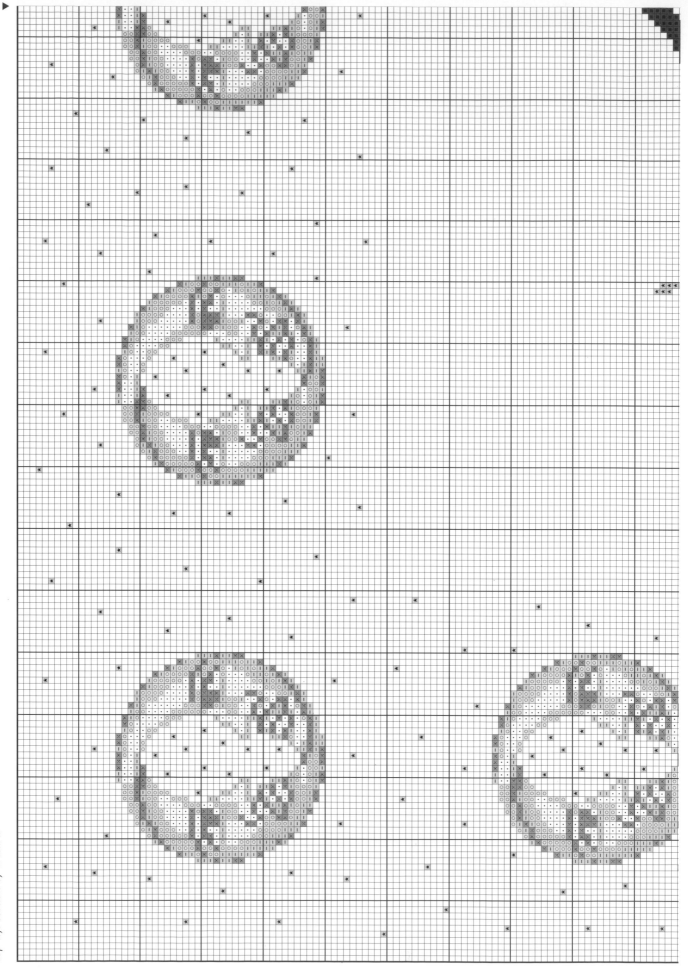

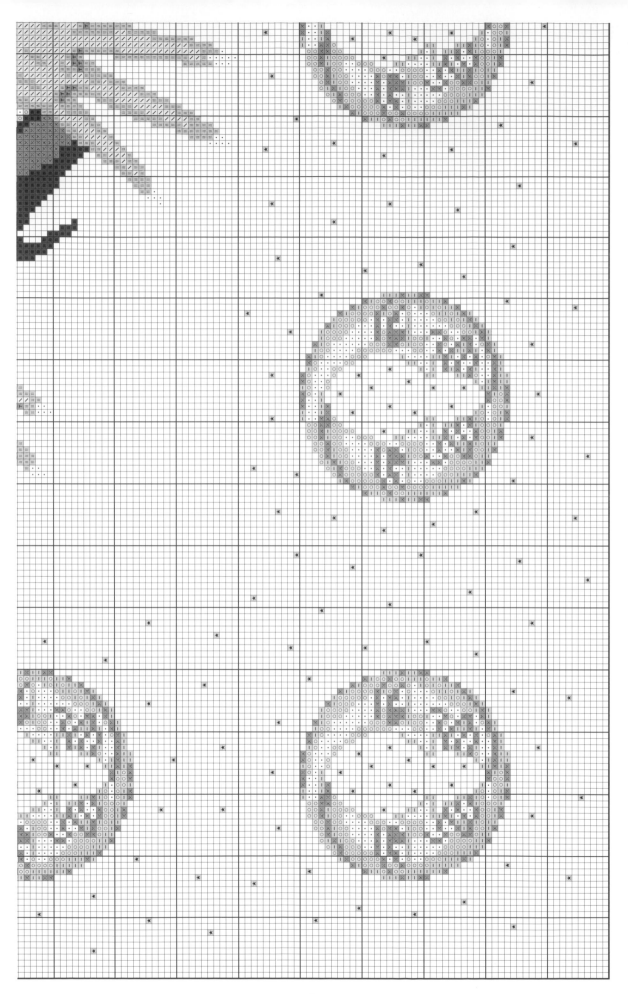

Bottom left section of Wizard

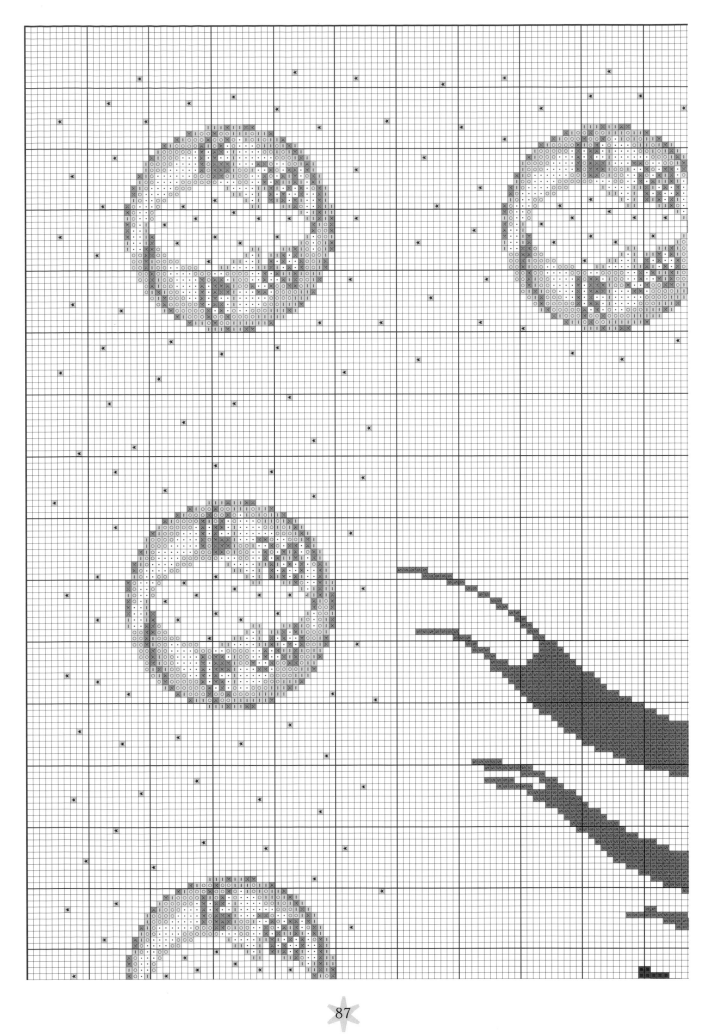

Top right section of Wizard

Viking Mythology

Over a thousand years ago, out of the harsh, cold north, a fierce race of tough, determined people swept across Europe, changing the communities they confronted for ever – the Vikings. Scourge of Christian lands, they came to plunder, to settle and to trade, bringing with them their own cults and gods.

✱ The Norsemen were a complex people – renowned for reckless destruction and cruelty, at the same time they were respected for courage, loyalty and determination. And their religion and its deities reflected this duality: Odin in Asgard ruled the warlike Aesir gods; whilst outside, the Vanir gods concerned themselves with fertility and agriculture, bringing peace and plenty to mankind. The tales of the gods are full of trickery and violence, but also of strength, humour and clear sightedness. Born in aggressive and turbulent times it was a faith that was rooted deeply in its culture and lasted for well over a thousand years.

Wall Hangings of the Gods

Frey, his sister Freyja and father Njord were Vanir fertility gods who went to live with the Aesir. Frey's name means 'Lord', and he was known as the guardian of the sacred wheat field. Along with Odin and Thor, he was one of the major Norse gods. Sif, of the wondrous golden hair, was Thor's wife. Her beautiful hair was once cut off as a joke by Loki, the trickster of the gods, who was forced by Thor to have new hair spun out of gold by the dwarves.

Telling the Runes
The runic alphabet was an Old Germanic writing system used widely in northern Europe from about the third century BC. Inscribed in wood, metal and stone, the letter forms were made of straight lines and sharp angles. Runes – the

name means 'mystery' and 'secret' in Old Germanic – were mainly used symbolically and were very important in ritual and magic. Eventually used solely for charms and memorial inscriptions, by the seventeenth century they gave way to the Latin alphabet. About 4,000 runic inscriptions have survived, mainly in Scandinavia. The rune stone accompanying Frey is the sign of the warrior, and signifies victory in battle. The rune stone accompanying Sif, depicts the fertility sign. The runes are charted so that you may stitch them as part of the wall hangings.

For each wall hanging, you will need:
- ✱ Two 1.3cm (½in) brass curtain rods, 38cm (15in) long
- ✱ Four fancy brass curtain rod ends
- ✱ Red or blue Linda fabric, 27-count, 57 x 31.5cm (22½ x 12½in)
- ✱ Black lightweight cotton backing fabric, 57 x 31.5cm (22½ x 12½in)
- ✱ DMC stranded cotton (floss) in the colours listed on the chart
- ✱ Matching sewing thread
- ✱ Tapestry needle, No 26
- ✱ Red or blue 5mm (¼in) cord, 76cm (30in)

All measurements include a 1.5cm (⅝in) seam allowance

1 Prepare your fabric, find the starting point (see page 10) then, following the Frey chart on pages 94 to 97, or the Sif chart on pages 98 to 101, work the design downwards. Use one strand of stranded cotton (floss).

2 When you have completed the embroidery, place it face down on a soft cloth or towel and press it carefully (see page 122).

3 Place the embroidered fabric face up on a firm, flat surface and place the lining fabric on top, right sides facing. Pin and tack (baste) together along the long edges and one short edge.

4 Machine stitch all round, leaving the short top edge open for turning. Remove pins and tacking (basting) stitches.

5 Press the seams open, trim any excess fabric from the corners, turn to the right side and press. Turn in the seam allowance on the top edge, and slip stitch together. Turn over a 4cm (1½ in) hem at the top and bottom edges and slip stitch in place, making casements for the curtain rods to go through. Stitch the cord into place round the curtain rod for hanging.

Rune stone motifs from the Frey and Sif charts on pages 95 and 99 are featured here in a selection of Framecraft products. The embroideries shown in the hairbrush and miniature brass frame are stitched on 22-count Hardanger fabric using one strand of stranded cotton (floss). The embroideries featured in the large greetings card and 12.5cm x 9cm (5 x 3½in) wooden frame, are stitched on 18-count Aida fabric using two strands of stranded cotton (floss).

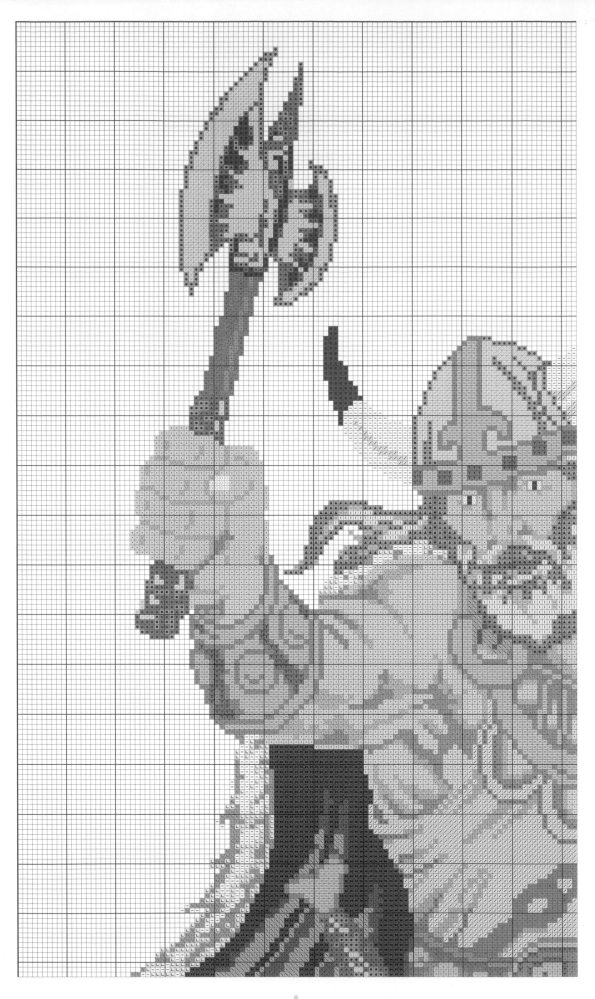

*Top left section
of Frey*

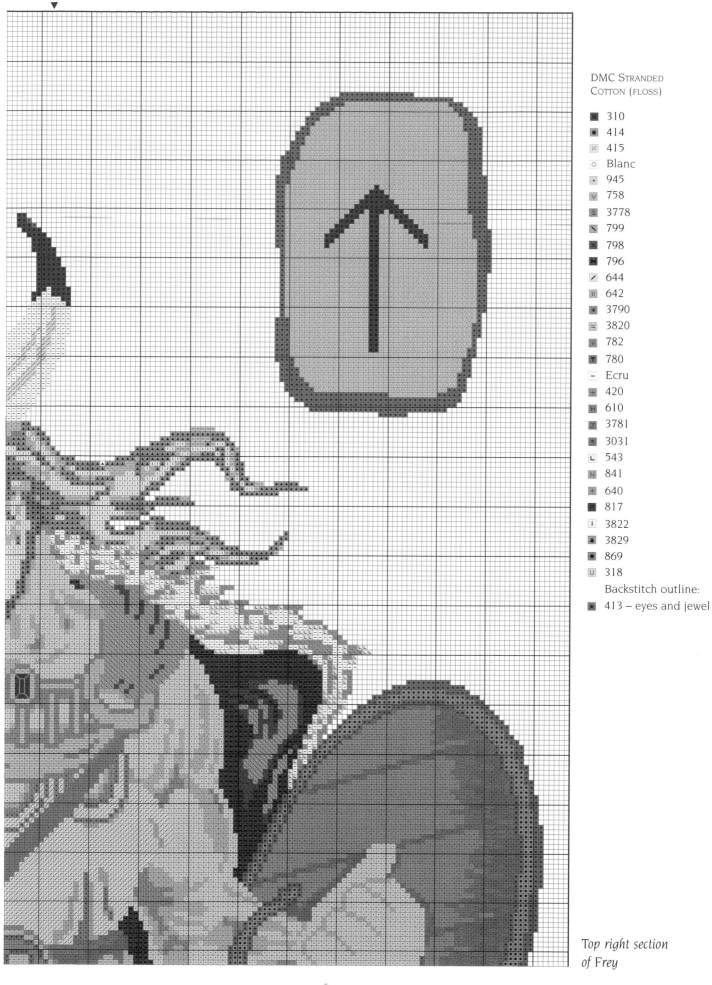

DMC Stranded
Cotton (floss)

- ■ 310
- ● 414
- ⁄ 415
- ○ Blanc
- · 945
- V 758
- S 3778
- N 799
- ✕ 798
- ✕ 796
- ⁄ 644
- ‖ 642
- ✱ 3790
- = 3820
- S 782
- T 780
- – Ecru
- ✿ 420
- H 610
- Z 3781
- ⁴ 3031
- L 543
- N 841
- + 640
- ✕ 817
- I 3822
- ▲ 3829
- ◆ 869
- U 318

Backstitch outline:
- ★ 413 – eyes and jewel

Top right section
of Frey

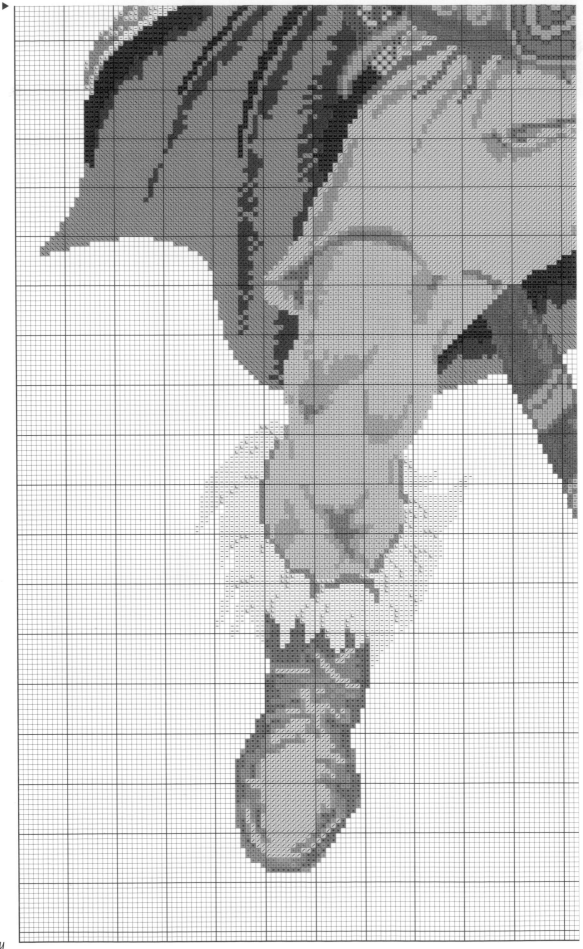

*Bottom left
section of Frey*

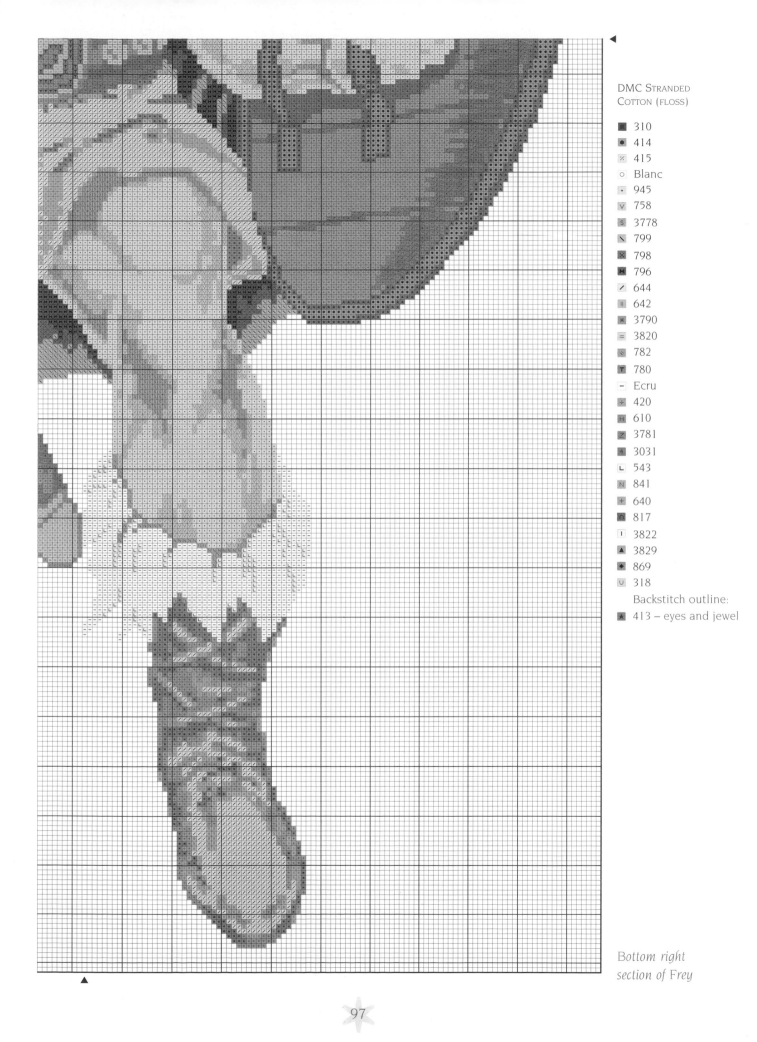

DMC STRANDED
COTTON (FLOSS)

- ■ 310
- ● 414
- ⊠ 415
- ○ Blanc
- · 945
- ∨ 758
- ⒮ 3778
- ⟍ 799
- ⊠ 798
- ⋈ 796
- ╱ 644
- ‖ 642
- ✳ 3790
- = 3820
- ⒮ 782
- T 780
- − Ecru
- ⊹ 420
- H 610
- Z 3781
- ◢ 3031
- L 543
- N 841
- ✛ 640
- ⌂ 817
- I 3822
- ▲ 3829
- ◆ 869
- U 318

Backstitch outline:
- ★ 413 – eyes and jewel

*Bottom right
section of Frey*

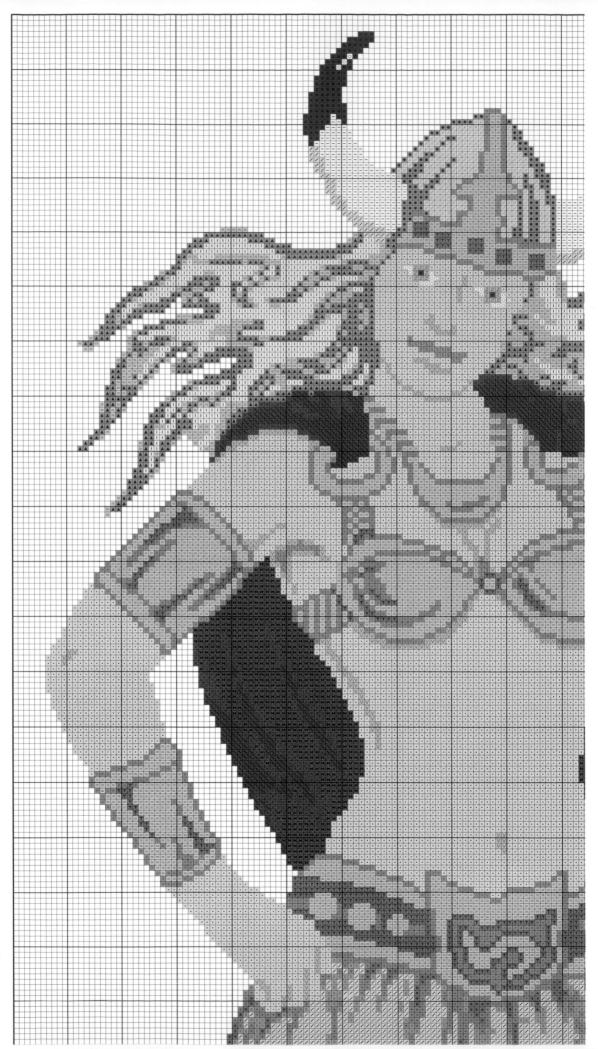

*Top left section
of Sif*

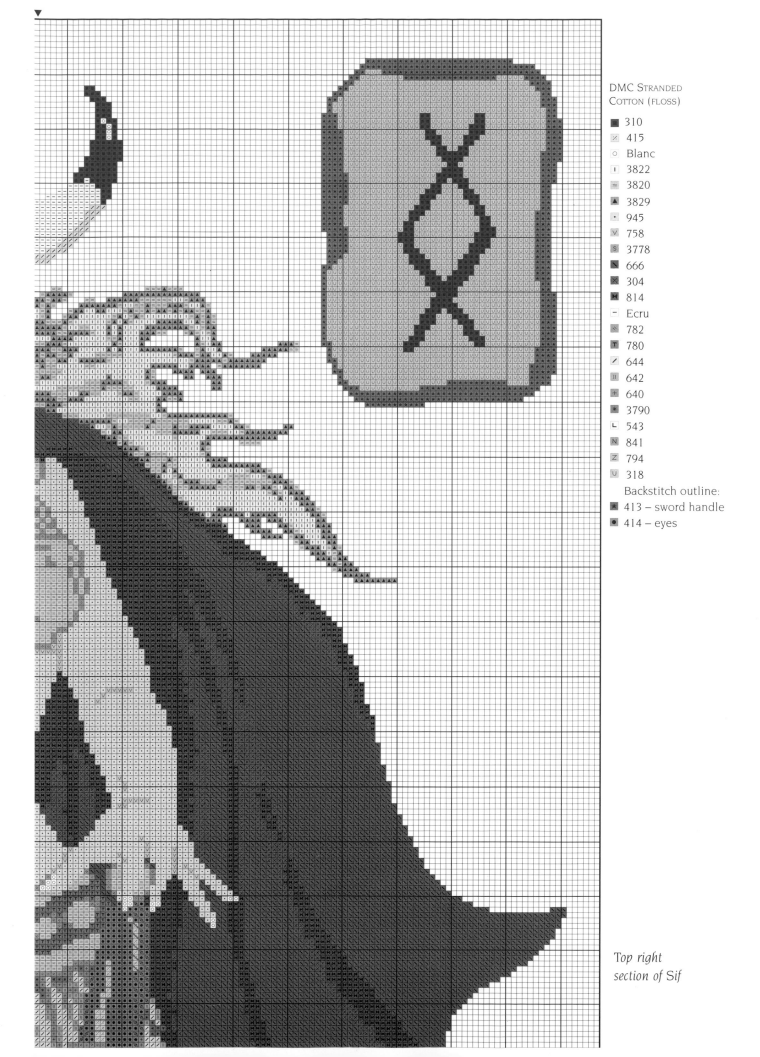

DMC STRANDED
COTTON (FLOSS)

- ■ 310
- ✠ 415
- ○ Blanc
- ı 3822
- = 3820
- ▲ 3829
- • 945
- V 758
- S 3778
- ◣ 666
- ✕ 304
- ◪ 814
- ⁻ Ecru
- ◩ 782
- ◪ 780
- ╱ 644
- ‖ 642
- ✚ 640
- ✳ 3790
- L 543
- N 841
- Z 794
- U 318

Backstitch outline:
- ★ 413 – sword handle
- ● 414 – eyes

*Top right
section of Sif*

Mermaid

Travellers' tales were once strewn with sightings of mermaids and mermen, fabulous marine beings, half-human, half-fish, with magical and prophetic powers. Though they could be kindly, merpeople were usually dangerous: their gifts brought misfortune, and they could cause floods and disasters. Beautiful and beguiling, they loved music and often sang bewitching songs that hypnotised unwary listeners, sometimes luring mortals to death by drowning.

✱ Although mermaids and mermen have been sighted on voyages to exotic parts of the world, they seem to prefer the cold water and rugged coastlines of Britain and Ireland, and the cliffs and fiords of Scandinavia. Some tales tell how they originated on the coast of Brittany and swam across the English Channel to Cornwall, where they were given their Anglo-French names meaning sea-maid and sea-men. They then spread up the west coast of the British Isles around northern Scotland to Scandinavia.

MERMAID FRAMED PICTURE

There is nothing more beautiful than the sight of a mermaid sitting on a rock, combing out her wonderful, long hair – and this beautiful mermaid is so realistic, she could tempt you right into the sea. But beware – her looks could belie a callous nature, and her smile might hide a selfish desire!

But if you're convinced she's friendly, she would look lovely in a bathroom, especially accompanied by the sea shell motifs.

✱ Navy Aida fabric, 18-count, 56 x 51cm (22 x 20in)
✱ DMC stranded cotton (floss) in the colours listed on the chart
✱ Kreinik blending filament in the colours on the chart
✱ Tapestry needle, No 26

✱ Firm mounting board, 45.5 x 40.5cm (18 x 16in)
✱ Masking tape
✱ Picture frame of your choice

1 Prepare your fabric, find the starting point (see page 10) then, following the Mermaid chart on pages 104 to 107, work the design downwards. Use two strands of stranded cotton (floss), and one strand for the backstitch, adding the blending filament where directed.

2 When you have completed the embroidery, place it face down on a soft cloth or towel and press it carefully (see page 122).

3 See 'Mounting embroideries for framing' on page 124 to mount and frame the finished embroidery.

The mermaid design would look perfectly at home in the bathroom. And you can use the border motifs from the sections of chart on pages 106 and 107 to add some perfect finishing touches. Towels take on a whole new identity when you add an embroidered Aida band. Turn a plain and ordinary towel into something special with the shell designs from the border. Worked in two strands of stranded cotton (floss) on a 6cm (2½in) woven edge band, picking up the colour of the towel. Brighten up your bathroom with a pot pourri jar, covered with a Framecraft jar lacy, embroidered using two strands of stranded cotton (floss), with a shell motif from the border.

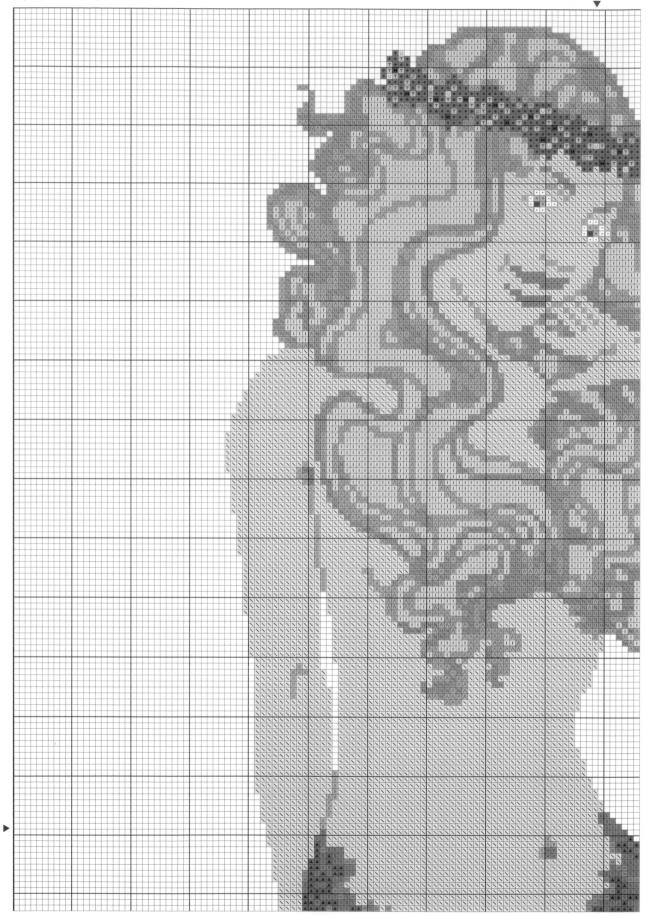

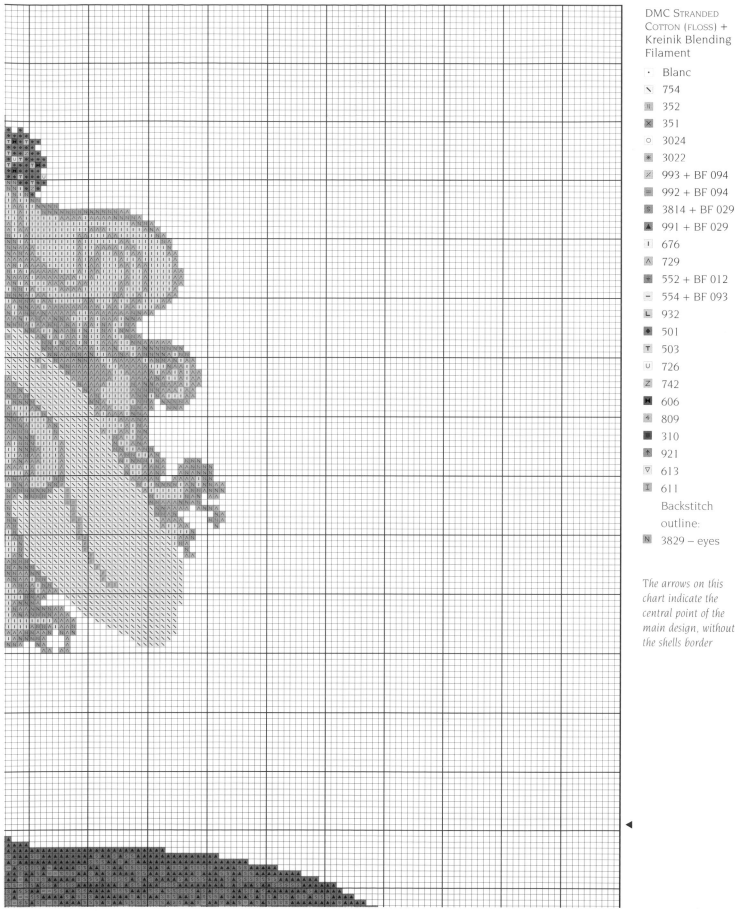

DMC STRANDED
COTTON (FLOSS) +
Kreinik Blending
Filament

· Blanc
\ 754
∥ 352
✕ 351
○ 3024
✳ 3022
⊘ 993 + BF 094
☰ 992 + BF 094
S 3814 + BF 029
▲ 991 + BF 029
I 676
∧ 729
✛ 552 + BF 012
– 554 + BF 093
L 932
◆ 501
T 503
U 726
Z 742
⋈ 606
4 809
▦ 310
↑ 921
▽ 613
I 611

Backstitch
outline:
N 3829 – eyes

*The arrows on this
chart indicate the
central point of the
main design, without
the shells border*

Greek Mythology

Modern European culture is heavily indebted to Greek myth and legend.
The ancient stories have inspired great artists, dramatists and novelists for hundreds
of years, and continue to do so. Taken to Italy early on, they were absorbed and
re-told by the Romans; names changed but the events stayed more or less the same.
Christianity might have swept away pagan belief, but Mount Olympus is still the
home of the gods where mighty Zeus is king; Pan plays his pipes; and Baccus
gets uproariously drunk.

✱   The gods of classical antiquity were not remote, perfect beings. In fact, they were very human-like, with intense passions and failings. They were often selfish and jealous, and notorious for their infidelity. Many a mortal was destroyed because they attracted their enmity. As well as the immortal gods, the mythology is peopled with monsters, heroes and giants.

ℱRAMED PICTURE OF NESSOS

Many Greek vases, bowls and amphorae were decorated with mythological scenes in a powerful, stylised form that illustrated the epic tales with dramatic simplicity. This effect transposes well into cross stitch – for instance, this striking design showing the centaur Nessos, is taken from a seventh century BC amphora.

Unlike the wise centaur Chiron, Nessos had a wicked and deceitful heart, and was the cause of the great hero Herakles' tragic death.

✱ Lemon Aida fabric, 14-count, 54.5 x 48cm (21½ x 19in)
✱ DMC stranded cotton (floss) in the colours listed on the chart
✱ Tapestry needle, No 24
✱ Firm mounting board, 44.5 x 38cm (17½ x 15in)
✱ Masking tape
✱ Picture frame of your choice

1 Prepare your fabric, find the starting point (see page 10) then, following the chart on pages 110 and 111, work the design downwards. Use two strands of stranded cotton (floss).

2 When you have completed the embroidery, press it carefully (see page 122).

3 See 'Mounting embroideries for framing' on page 122 to mount and frame the finished embroidery.

𝒯HE OLYMPIANS

THE TWELVE CHIEF GODS OF GREEK MYTHOLOGY

ZEUS	the head of the gods and spiritual father of gods and people
HERA	Zeus' wife, the queen of heaven and guardian of marriage
HEPHAESTUS	god of fire and metal workers
ATHENA	goddess of wisdom and war
APOLLO	god of light, poetry and music
ARTEMIS	goddess of wildlife and the moon
ARES	god of war
APHRODITE	goddess of love
HESTIA	goddess of the hearth
HERMES	messenger of the gods and ruler of science and invention
POSEIDON	ruler of the sea
DEMETER	goddess of agriculture

The border from the Centaur design can be worked separately as shown here as a shelf border. The design is embroidered on to a 5cm (2in) Aida band using two strands of stranded cotton (floss).

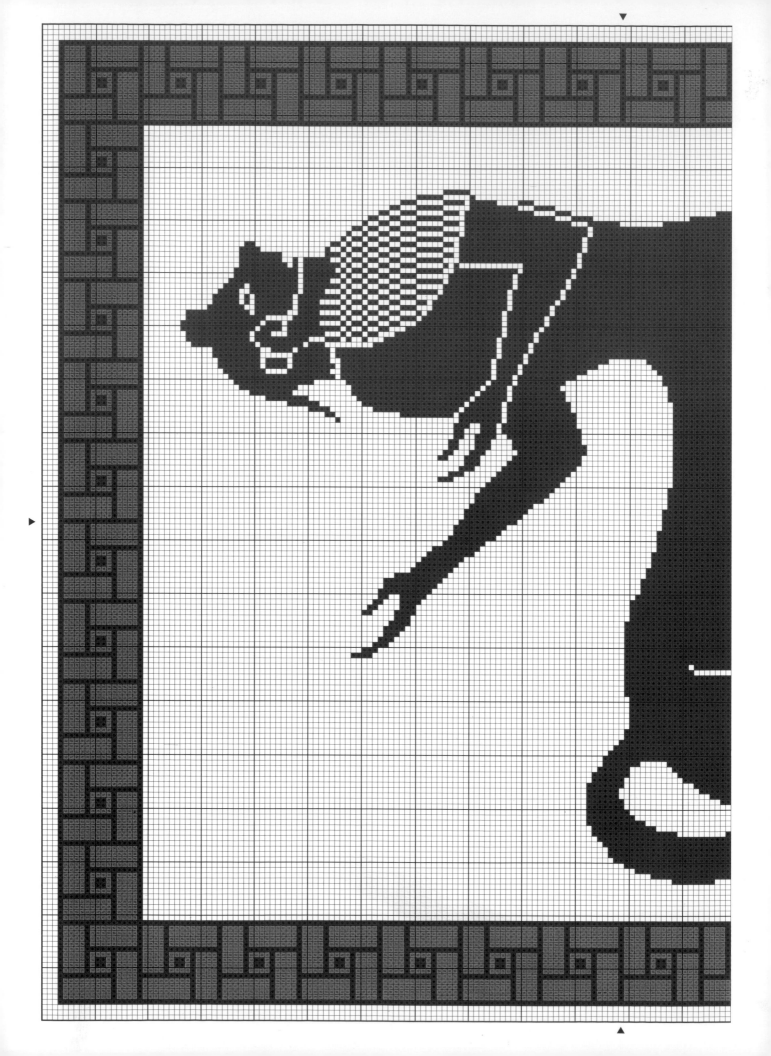

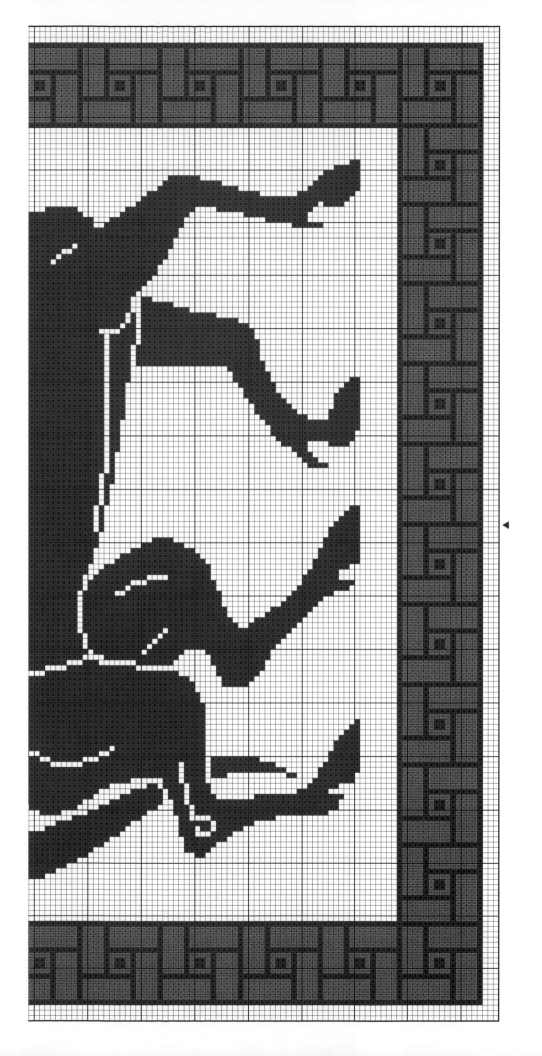

DMC Stranded
Cotton (floss)

■ 310
▨ 920

Symbol Library

This section contains all manner of talismans and symbols used from the earliest times to the middle ages, as well as some modern day ones. Altogether, thirty-five are charted, among them ancient Egyptian symbols, Christian monograms, Chinese symbols and rune stones. All the symbols are shown as stitched pieces (see pages 112 and 113), and are accompanied by explanatory text. For advice on which threads and fabrics to use see the captions on page 114. As you will see, they have visual as well as symbolic beauty.

The exquisite symbol designs featured on pages 116 to 121 are all embroidered on fine 18-count Aida fabric, using two strands of stranded cotton (floss), and set in Framecraft products. Making up instructions for the trinket box lids, paperweights, and miniature brass frames can be found in the 'Displaying Your Work' section starting on page 122. The Anchor Cross and the Lyre from page 118 are embroidered on 18-count Aida fabric using two strands of stranded cotton (floss), and mounted in DMC studio card mounts with 5cm (2in) cut-outs. The framed pictures pictured opposite show off the symbols to their best when stitched on a dark background.

✱ Use the library to create meaningful hand-stitched gifts, matching the symbolism of the design to the person or event you are celebrating.

1 St Bridget's Cross – traditional symbol of protection.

2 A variation of the Anchor Cross – Christian symbol for hope.

3 The Swastika or Fylfot – represents a cross with flames streaming from its ends. A very old symbol, believed to date back to prehistoric times. Symbol for the sun, the highest god, power and life force.

4 The anti-nuclear emblem, or peace symbol.

5 One of several symbolising the art of alchemy. The sun sign at the centre is surrounded by the four elemental triangles and crowned with the Christian cross, all inside a circle which represents the eternal or spiritual dimension and its endless possibilities.

6 The Crossed Cross – world evangelisation. The central cross represents the four points of the compass; the small crosses represent the spread of the Christian faith in all four directions.

7 Healing talisman – incorporates the divine monogrammaton with the solar imagery of Raphael, archangel of healing. Said to be amazingly effective in both preventing and curing all manner of sickness. Traditionally struck on gold, or inscribed on parchment.

8 The god-form Khopri, traditionally depicted as a beetle – most common of Egyptian talismans symbolising the emergence of new life from inert matter. Shown in the centre of a circle formed by a snake devouring its own tail, again, symbolising the perpetual self-renewal of nature.

9 The Creator's Star or Star of David – represents the six days of creation. Also a symbol of Zionism.

10 The Anchor Cross – used by early Christians as a secret symbol of their faith.

11 The Ten Commandments – the tablets of stone Moses brought back from Mount Sinai.

12 Grapes – the sacrament of Holy Communion.

13 Crown – Christ as King of Kings.

14 Butterfly – the resurrection and life everlasting for the believer.

15 Thistle – earthly sorrow and sin, and the sufferings of Christ.

16 Ship with the cross as the mast – the church with Christ as the captain.

17 Alpha and Omega – the first and last letters of the Greek alphabet, standing for Christ who says, `I am Alpha and Omega – the beginning and the ending'.

18 Lyre – David and his musical abilities. Also joy in praising the Lord.

19 Sign for Aum – the greeting of peace in India; the four states of consciousness: awake, dreaming, sleeping without dreams, and the transcendental state.

20 Yin-yang – from Chinese philosophy and cosmology. The world's most basic relationships represented as a balancing act between two opposing life forces, yin (the white) and yang (the black).

21 The Caduceus, Wand of Mercury, the Rod of Healing and of Peace – a mystic talisman, a powerful mascot healing quarrels, driving away sickness and giving eloquence and youthfulness to its possessor.

22 The Cross over the Globe – world evangelisation.

23 Fu – a Chinese symbol for authority, divine power, and the ability to judge between right and wrong.

24 Nirvana – the mystical perception of godliness and truth, or non-attachment.

25 Dove with Olive Branch – peace.

26 A return or a coming back – from earliest Chinese writings.

27 Jerusalem Cross or Cross of Palestine – the kingdom of Jerusalem, and the unity of all Christians.

28 Cornucopia or Horn of Plenty – promotes success in business and general prosperity.

29 Autumn – an old Germanic time sign.

30 Bamboo with seven knots – a well known Hindu talisman, that gives wisdom and power. The circle is the symbol of Eternity, the triangles stand for the Hindu Trinity, the Serpent for wisdom, and the bamboo for the seven degrees of learning the devout must possess.

31 Viking Rune of The Self – man, the human race.

32 Viking Rune of Joy – joy, absence of suffering and sorrow.

33 Viking Rune of Growth – associated with the fertility cult, symbolising rebirth, new life.

34 The Udjat – an important Egyptian symbol named after the 'sound eye' of Horus. Regarded as a powerful, protective amulet.

35 The Ankh – creation; found from earliest times in Egyptian art.

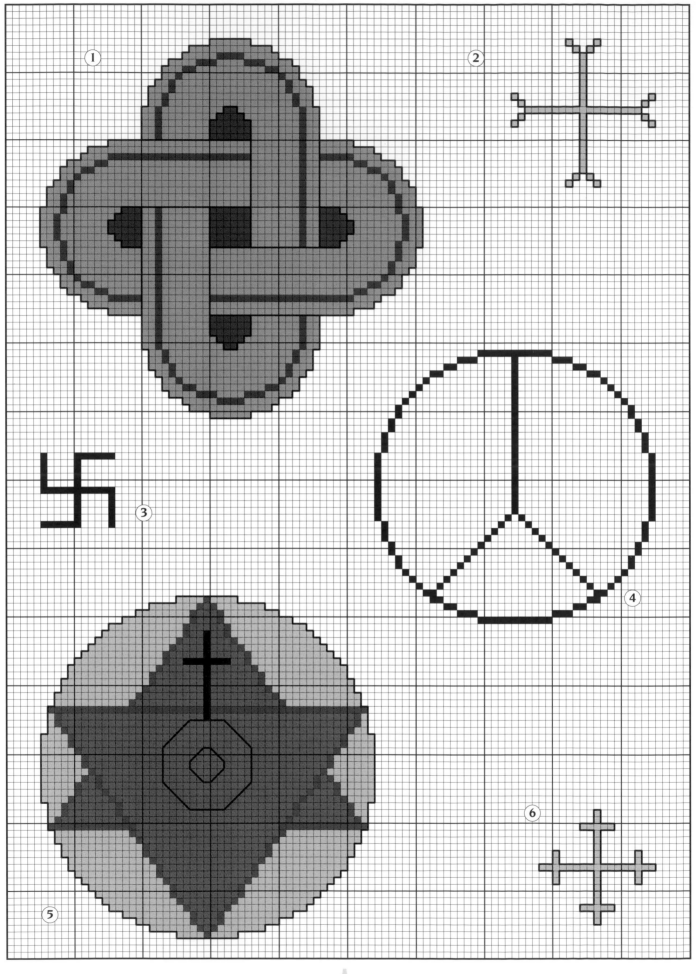

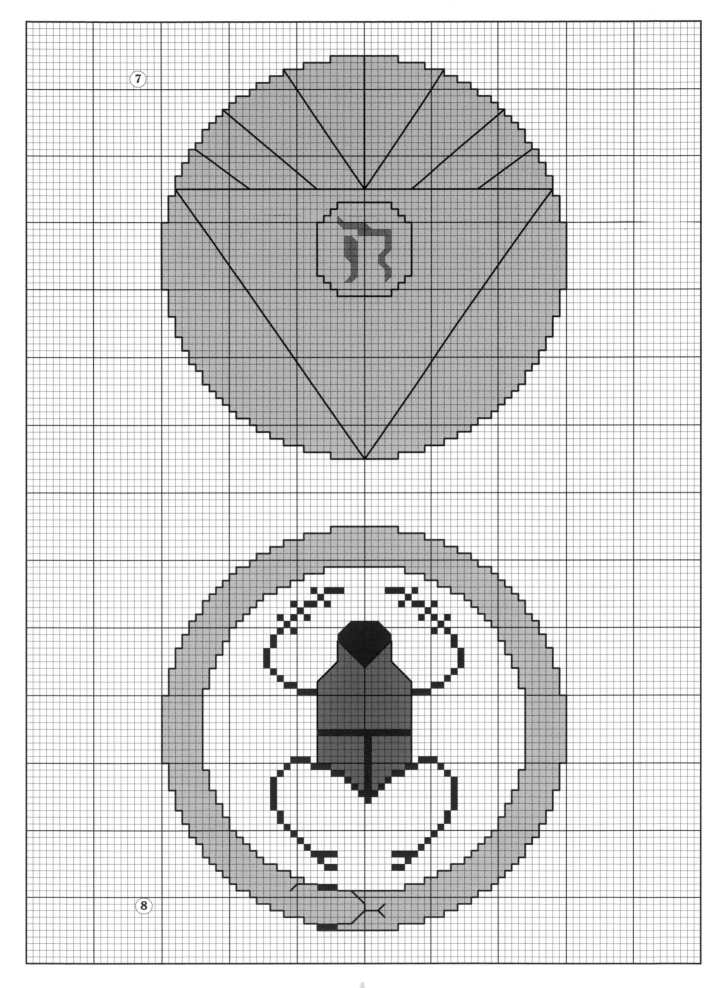

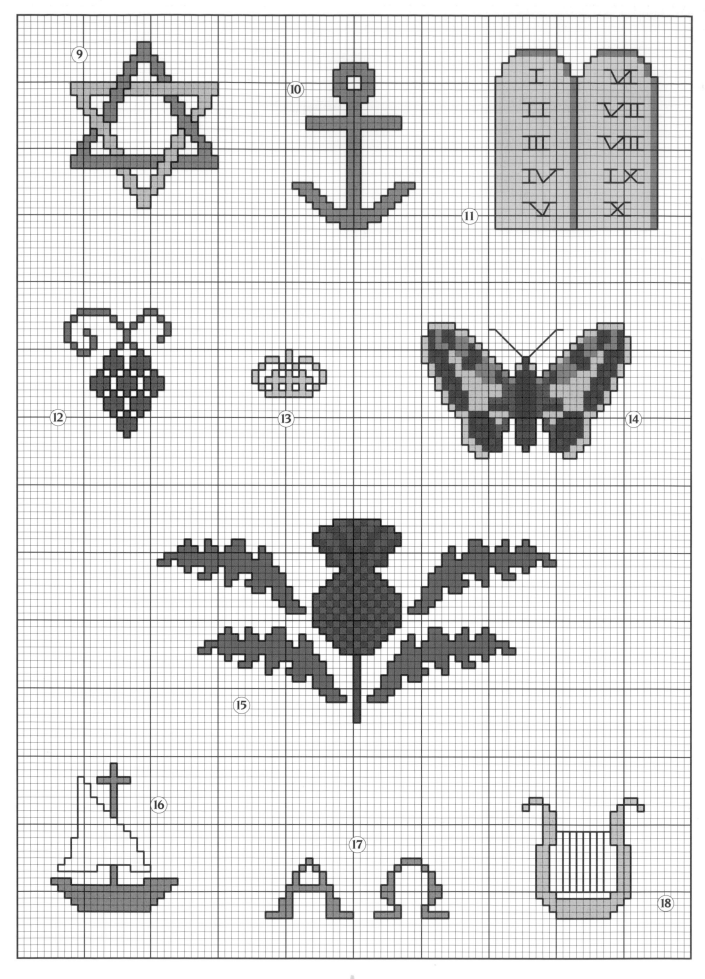

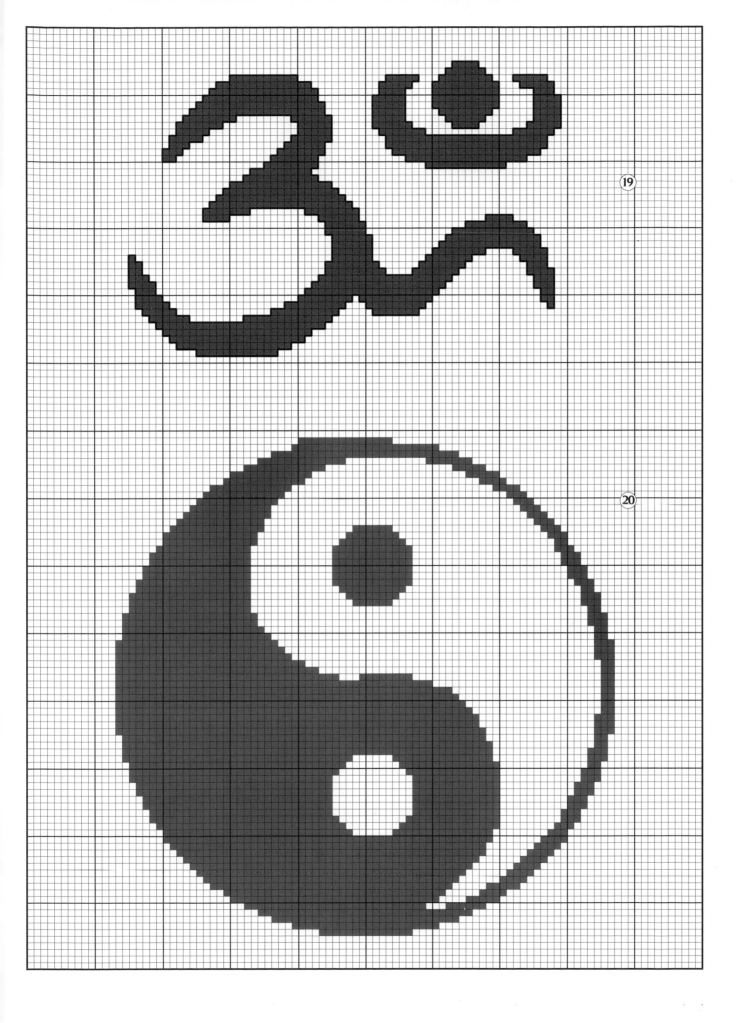

19

20

Finishing Techniques

When you have spent many hours lovingly embroidering your design, it would be a shame to spoil the finished work by careless pressing or laundering, or by not displaying it to its best advantage. Within this section, you'll find guidelines on how to press a cross stitch embroidery, how to care for it and how best to frame or display it.

PRESSING

When you have completed your cross stitch embroidery, it will need to be pressed so that it is flat for mounting and framing. To protect your work, place right side down on to a soft towel and cover the reverse side with a thin, slightly damp cloth. Press the embroidery with a hot iron. Take care not to flatten the stitches.

MOUNTING EMBROIDERIES FOR FRAMING

Before it can be framed, your embroidery will have to be stretched tightly over mounting board.

1 Cut your mounting board 2.5–4cm (1–1½in) smaller all around than your needlework fabric. Place the embroidery face down on to a clean flat surface and place the mounting board centrally on to it.

2 Fold one edge of the fabric over the mounting board (ensuring that it is perfectly straight) and secure it with pins along the edge of the board. Secure the opposite edge in the same way, making sure that the fabric is straight and taut on the board.

3 Use masking tape to secure the edges of the fabric on to the back of the mounting board, and then remove the pins. Repeat this procedure on the remaining two edges.

If you think that this procedure is a little bit too fiddly to attempt, a company called Press-On Products Inc. have brought out a wonderful range of self-stick mounting boards in five different sizes, available from most large department stores and good craft shops. These really are a treat to work with, and make the job very easy. You simply cut the board to size as before, peel off the backing, lay your needlework fabric on to the board making sure it is centred and when you are completely satisfied, press down very hard over the entire needlework surface. Tape the excess fabric to the back of the mounting board with masking tape.

Your embroidery picture is now ready to be framed. The best result will be achieved if you take it to a professional framer. If you are having glass in your frame, you will get an improved effect if you have non-reflective glass. Although it is slightly more expensive it is well worth it.

DISPLAYING YOUR WORK

There are many lovely ways to display your work, and I hope the projects throughout the book have inspired you to try something different. This chapter focuses on the ready-made settings available from good craft suppliers (see suppliers list, page 127). Most of them call for small designs, so if you want to work more than one at a time, economise on fabric by cutting a piece large enough to sew several designs on rather than cutting a small piece for each one. Remember to space them well.

GREETING CARDS

Personalised greetings cards containing a small embroidery are a pleasure to make and to receive – a wonderful way of showing someone that you care. These cards will be treasured long after shop bought ones have been forgotten.

There are many types of card mounts on the market, but the basic methods of assembly are the same.

✱ Cross stitch fabric slightly smaller than the card mount you wish to use

✱ Chosen greetings card mount

✱ Embroidery threads as listed for each design

✱ Ultra-soft, medium weight iron-on interfacing (optional)

✱ Double sided adhesive tape

1 Work the cross stitch embroidery in the centre of your fabric.

2 When completed, press, then iron the interfacing on to the wrong side of your fabric to prevent it from fraying.

3 Next, centre the design in the card 'window'. Use double-sided tape to fix the design into the card and press the backing down firmly.

TRINKET BOXES AND BOWLS

There is a wide range of commercially available trinket boxes and bowls for displaying cross stitch embroideries. They are available in metal finishes including brass and silver plate, cut glass, coloured porcelain, enamel and wood. They make an attractive and useful gift, and look lovely whether displayed on a dressing table or mantle piece.

✱ Cross stitch fabric slightly larger than the lid of your chosen trinket box or bowl

✱ Trinket box or bowl of your choice

✱ Embroidery threads as listed for each design

✱ Ultra-soft, medium weight iron-on interfacing (optional)

✱ Soft pencil

✱ Craft adhesive

CROSS STITCH AFTER-CARE

You may find at some stage that your cross stitch projects need to be laundered. This is no problem: just follow the simple advice which is specially recommended by DMC in conjunction with their stranded cotton (floss).

WASHING

Cotton or linen fabric
Wash separately from all other laundry, by hand in warm, soapy water.
Rinse thoroughly. Squeeze without twisting and hang out to dry.
Iron on reverse side using two layers of white linen.

Synthetic fabric
Not recommended

BLEACHING OR WHITENING AGENT

Cotton or linen fabric
Dilute product according to manufacturer's instructions.
Pre-soak the embroidery in clear water, then soak for five minutes in a solution of about one tablespoon of disinfectant per litre (2pt) of cold water.
Rinse thoroughly in cold water.

Synthetic fabric
If the white of the fabric is not of a high quality, follow the above instructions. If it is a pure white (white with a bluish tinge) do not use bleaching or whitening agent.

DRY CLEANING

Cotton or linen fabric
Avoid dry cleaning.
Some spot removers (benzene, trichloroethylene) can be used for small stains.

Synthetic fabric
NOT RECOMMENDED, even for a small occasional stain.

1 Work the cross stitch embroidery in the centre of your fabric.

2 When completed, press, then iron the interfacing on to the wrong side of your fabric to prevent it from fraying.

3 Place the embroidery face up on a firm, flat surface. Gently remove all parts from the trinket box or bowl lid. Use the rim of the lid to centre the design. Then draw around the outer edge on to the fabric using a soft pencil. Remove the lid and cut the fabric to size.

4 Replace the clear acetate and place your design into the lid, with the right side to the acetate. Place the sponge behind and push the metal locking disc firmly into place, with the raised side of the disc facing the sponge. When the locking disc is tightly in position, use craft adhesive to secure the flock lid lining card to it.

PAPERWEIGHTS
Paperweights make unusual gifts, which can be put to practical use on a desk or used as ornaments round the home.

* Cross stitch fabric slightly larger than your chosen paperweight
* Framecraft paperweight of your choice
* Embroidery threads as listed for each design
* Ultra-soft, medium weight, iron-on interfacing (optional)

1 Work the cross stitch embroidery in the centre of your fabric.

2 When completed, press, then iron the interfacing on to the wrong side of your fabric to prevent it from fraying.

3 Place the embroidery on a firm, flat surface and use the paper template provided with the paperweight to draw round your design, making sure it is centred. Cut the fabric to size and place it right side down into the recess on the base of the paperweight.

4 Place the paper template on the reverse side of your embroidery. Peel away the backing from the protective base and carefully stick it to the base of the paperweight. Make sure that the embroidery and the template do not move out of place.

MINIATURE BRASS & SILVER PLATED FRAMES
The miniature frames now available for cross stitch embroideries are inexpensive, easy to assemble, and give a professional look to your work. They make an excellent – and less expensive – alternative to having your work professionally framed.

* Cross stitch fabric slightly larger than the frame you wish to use
* Miniature frame of your choice
* Embroidery threads as listed for each design
* Ultra-soft, medium weight iron-on interfacing (optional)

1 Work the cross stitch embroidery in the centre of your fabric.

2 When completed, press, then iron the interfacing on to the wrong side of your fabric to prevent it from fraying.

3 Carefully dismantle all parts of the frame, and use the template provided to draw around your design, making sure that it is centred. Cut the fabric to size.

4 Replace the clear acetate and place your design centred into the frame with the right side towards the acetate, followed by the cardboard template, and finally the backing. Secure the backing using the pins provided.

JEWELLERY FRAMES
Framecraft miniatures produce a beautiful range of jewellery frames in a variety of different finishes, in which to display small embroidered designs. These can make ideal personalised gifts for someone special.

* Cross stitch fabric slightly larger than your chosen jewellery frame
* Jewellery frame of your choice
* Embroidery threads as listed for each design
* Ultra-soft, medium weight iron-on interfacing (optional)
* Craft adhesive
* Soft pencil

1 Work the cross stitch embroidery in the centre of your fabric.

2 When completed, press, then iron the interfacing on to the wrong side of your fabric to prevent it from fraying.

3 Place the finished embroidery face up on a firm, flat surface. Gently remove all parts from the jewellery frame. Place the acetate over your embroidery, repositioning it until you are sure that the design is in the centre. Draw around the outer edge of the acetate using a soft pencil to make an outline on the fabric. Next, remove the acetate, and cut the fabric to size, following the pencil outline.

4 Replace the clear acetate and place your design centred into the frame with the right side to the acetate. Place the sponge behind, and push the metal locking disc firmly into place using thumb pressure, with the raised side of the disc facing the sponge. When the locking disc is tightly in position, use a little craft adhesive to secure the flock backing disc to it. Bend the lugs on the frame over to the back of the flock backing disc.

The zodiac designs above are (clockwise from top left) Virgo and Gemini pictures, Scorpio and Libra cards, Capricorn, Scorpio and Cancer designs, Taurus box, zodiac pendants and Cancer window hanging.

125

Acknowledgements

I would like to give my thanks to the following people for their skilful sewing up of the cross stitch embroideries in this book: Diana Hewitt, Lesley Buckerfield, Maureen Hipgrave, Lynda Potter, Jenny Whitlock, Judy Riggans, Andrea Martin, Libby Shaw, Rita Boulton, Pat Chapman, Holly Jenkins, Paloma Allen, Jeane Williams and Angela Taylor. And for the making up of the projects, Connie Woolcott. Thank you, ladies, for your lovely work and your loyalty over the years. It is much appreciated.

Many thanks also to Tom Aird for the skilful mounting of the embroideries, and excellent framing service over the last twelve years.

I would also like to thank the following companies who have contributed embroidery threads, fabrics and accessories, for use in this book: Framecraft Miniatures Ltd, DMC Creative World Ltd, Kreinik Mfg Co Inc, Mac Gregor Designs.

Charted designs reproduced in conjunction with Crafted Software.

Zodiac designs from original paintings by Leannda Cross. Thanks Leannda, they make the book look beautiful!

Suppliers

Framecraft Miniatures Ltd manufacture an extensive range of small frames, miniature boxes, jewellery, Crafta cards and many other products that can be completed with small cross stitch designs, making exquisite gifts. Also suppliers of Mill Hill beads.

Framecraft items and accessories are available from:

Framecraft Miniatures Ltd,
372–376 Summer Lane, Hockley,
Birmingham B19 3QA

Gay Bowles Sales Inc,
PO Box 1060, Janesville, WI 53547, USA

Ireland Needlecraft Pty Ltd,
Unit 4, 2–4 Keppel Drive, Hallam,
Victoria 3803, Australia

Anne Brinkley Designs Inc,
761 Palmer Avenue, Holmdel, NJ 97733, USA

The Embroidery Shop,
Greville-Parker, 252 Queen Street,
Masterton, New Zealand

Stranded embroidery cottons (floss), evenweave fabrics and other DMC products featured in this book are available from:

DMC Creative World Ltd,
Pullman Road, Wigston,
Leicester LE8 2DY

DMC Needlecraft Pty,
PO Box 317, Earlswood 2206,
New South Wales 2204, Australia

The DMC Corporation,
Port Kearney Bld, #10 South Kearney,
NJ 070732-0650, USA

Kreinik Mfg Co Inc manufacture specialist embroidery threads including Metallic Blending Filaments. Their products are available from:

Coats Crafts UK,
Mc Mullen Road,
Darlington, Co. Durham, DL1 1YQ

Fleur De Paris,
5835 Washington Blvd, Culver City, CA 90232, USA

Gay Bowles Sales Inc,
PO Box 1060, Janesville, WI 53547, USA

Ireland Needlecraft Pty Ltd,
Unit 4, 2–4 Keppel Drive, Hallam,
Victoria 3803, Australia

The Embroidery Shop,
Greville-Parker, 252 Queen Street, Masterton,
New Zealand

Serendipity Designs,
11301 International Drive, Richmond,
VA 23236, USA

L C Kramer,
2525 E. Burnside, Portland, OR 97214, USA

Wichelt Imports,
RR #1, Hwy. 35, Stoddard, WI 54658, USA

The trinket box on page 12 is available from:

Mac Gregor Designs,
PO Box 129,
Burton upon Trent DE14 3XH

Gold relief outliner is available from:

Philip and Tacey,
North Way, Andover SP10 5BA

Index